Advance Reviews for HEALING YOUR HABITS:

While reading the book, I kept thinking, "How wonderful," such a positive approach, such definite directions. I am excited to recommend this book. It has relevance not only to those who are having difficulty in "healing their habits," but also to those who want to improve the quality of their every day "problem solving."
    Pat Mazzola, R.N., B.A., C.C.E.

Realistic, encouraging, and empowering.
    Kathryn Katz, Ed.D.
    Assistant Professor, Health Education
    Hunter College, City University of New York

It's easy to stop a bad habit—the hard part is to *not start again*. HEALING YOUR HABITS focuses on preventing relapse, coping with those moments of weakness which derail so many plans. HEALING YOUR HABITS is a well-chosen title; addictive, out-of-control behavior can't be controlled very well by punishment and self-condemnation. It really requires inner healing, and this book offers genuine aid in that process.
    Christopher Gilbert, Ph.D.
    Clinical Psychologist

Highly recommended for its simplicity and comprehension.
    Joseph E. Grodjeks, D.D.S.
    Dentist

A realistic approach . . . Dr. Luciani helps readers to understand their problems before he introduces them to his workable, step-by-step program . . . Excellent for lay people and professionals.
    Patricia Smith, R.N., B.S.

Blends psychology and spirituality beautifully. Anyone who uses the easily learned techniques will overcome their addiction.
    Samuel E. Menahem, Ph. D.
    Director, Center for Psychotherapy and Spiritual Growth
    Fort Lee, New Jersey

HEALING YOUR HABITS

HEALING YOUR HABITS

INTRODUCING DIRECTED IMAGINATION

A successful technique for overcoming addictive problems

by Joseph J. Luciani, Ph.D.

San Diego, California

© Copyright 1990 LuraMedia
San Diego, California
International Copyright Secured
Publisher's Catalog Number LM-619
Printed and bound in the United States of America

Cover illustration by Carol Jeanotilla, Denver, CO

LuraMedia
7060 Miramar Road, Suite 104
San Diego, CA 92121

Library of Congress Cataloging-in-Publication Data

Luciani, Joseph J.

    Healing your habits : introducing directed imagination, a successful technique for overcoming addictive problems / by Joseph J. Luciani.
       p.   cm.
    ISBN 0-931055-71-7
    1. Compulsive behavior—Treatment. 2. Imagery (Psychology)—Therapeutic use.   I. Title.
    RC533.L83   1990
    616.85'2—dc20   90-30154
                                                          CIP

Dedicated
to my wife, Karen
my son, Justin
and my daughter, Lauren

Contents

	Preview	1
1	**Looking Ahead**	9
	■ A Program for Success	
2	**Recognizing the Characters of Your Habit**	25
	■ Directed Imagination	
3	**Dealing with the Stress of Habit Re-formation**	53
	■ Body Nurturing	
4	**Viewing Your Habit from Another Perspective**	71
	■ Journal	
5	**Changing Your Focus**	99
	■ Hypnosis	
	Checklists	129
6	**Establishing a Context**	137
	■ Psychological Autobiography	

PREVIEW

Some people seem to handle adversity well, always rising to the occasion in heroic fashion. We all know this type. They are the ones who are able to stick to a diet and actually lose the weight they set out to lose. They begin an exercise program and never miss a day. These are the same people who tell you that they have decided to quit smoking and, without batting an eye, throw away their last pack of cigarettes.

This book was never intended for them. This book is for those of you who cannot trust such heroic attributes to rise up in support of your efforts.

Some children grow up with a capability for handling life's pressures quite well; others, not so well. Whether because they were overwhelmed, overprotected, or overburdened, children who manage to escape and avoid life's early confrontations eventually pay a price. The child who knows only impotence never develops a sense of inner trust and conviction. When confronted with anxiety or tension, rather than looking inward for strength, this child seeks a strategy to deflect the discomfort. This quest to lessen discomfort invariably leads to the formation of specific behavioral strategies that, if reinforced, may result in addictive or habituated behavior.

Your Addiction Is Learned Behavior

Many of these strategies for handling pressure were adopted quite accidentally (notable exceptions, however, are cigarettes, alcohol, and most drugs; these particular substances are often sought out for either social acceptance or a medicinal desire to alter one's mood or to reduce anxiety). Imagine that your dog runs away. You spend the entire evening roaming the streets, calling for Fido. Frustrated and tired, you finally return home, only to find the door locked and Fido looking out at you from the window, excitedly wagging his tail. In order not to wake your spouse and your children, you decide to slip in through the basement window. Unfortunately the burglar alarm goes off. Just as your neighbor's lights begin to blink on, a police car pulls into your driveway.

Just as you begin to experience an anxiety melt-down, your hand comes across some M&M's stashed away in your pocket. Without giving it a second thought, you pop a few into your mouth. As you chomp down into the sweet chocolate, for the first time tonight something feels good. Each bite offers a bit of solace and comfort.

Certainly this one instance is not going to turn you into an M&M's junkie, but it will establish a connection that, if repeated a few more times, could become a pattern. Now if this pattern is combined with an inability, or an unwillingness, to handle stressful situations, then a full-fledged habit or addiction may develop. (A habit is any behavior that has become automatic; an addiction is a habit with the added dimension of physiological chemical dependence.) A similar scenario would hold true if, as a child, those same M&M's were associated with, say, special times at Grandma's house. After a particularly stressful encounter with the boss, you might find yourself stopping at a convenience store on the way home with an irresistible urge for those little chocolate goodies.

In these examples, the M&M's (or whatever habit you are trying to break) inadvertently become part of a strategy for reducing tension. And why should you not repeat these actions? What is so bad about a little candy pick-me-up? They do bring comfort, and there is nothing wrong with wanting a little comfort once in a while, is there?

The unfortunate problem is that these strategies or patterns, over time, become "have to's" rather than "want to's." There is no question that your initial desire was just to make life a little easier, a bit less stressful. But now these same habits and addictions, to which you once turned for relief, have become sources of stress — especially when you realize that you are no longer in control of your habit and are unable to quit.

If nothing else, it is absolutely critical for you to understand one fact about habits: *They were all learned.* As simplistic as this may sound, it is a very important and often overlooked point. Just as you learned that certain addictive strategies (e.g., pick up the phone, pick up a cigarette; turn on the television set, get a snack; get home from work, have a cocktail) served to rescue you from life's difficulties, or reward you for surviving them, you can be taught to unlearn these same patterns.

Incidentally, when referring to life's "difficulties," I include not only external stresses such as traffic jams or tax audits but also psychological stresses such as boredom, emptiness, and loneliness. Regardless of the initial motivation that spawned your addictive or habitual behavior, you can *learn* to replace the destructive thinking that has ensued with appropriate and healthy life choices that allow you to once again progress and grow.

Your current thinking has become an integral part of the habit or addiction from which you suffer. In a very real sense, as your will became compromised by the demands of your addictive behavior, your thinking became its accomplice. Do not misunderstand: Your will has not been destroyed. Quite the opposite is true. Your ability to take charge of your life and institute appropriate changes lies ready and waiting for you to unleash it. Your will has only been silenced, not impaired.

It is understandable that your thoughts have led to confusion, pessimism, and distrust of your ability to handle stress. You have probably been feeling overwhelmed and off-balance for a long time. This book will help you to corral these thoughts in such a way that you can finally confront them and dismantle their grip on your life. This goal is a reasonable expectation, not an exaggeration.

Your life was never meant to be regulated by an addictive substance, an obsessive worry, a phobia, or a compulsive habit. Try to realize that life, when lived appropriately, is a beautiful process of unfolding and expressing your nature. Could anyone not have a sense of awe and wonder at how a tiny acorn can one day yield a stately oak tree? Life, all life, is full of such expressions of grandeur. Within you is such a potential for expression, for fulfillment, for grandeur.

Destructive habits and addictions are obstacles to this development. They, like a sidewalk laid over an acorn, prevent the oak from sending its branches skyward. Such habits were not meant to be. They are interlopers and parasites that live off your vital life energy. Life's complications and pressures need to be accepted with confidence and courage. To avoid or reject the demands of life is to reject life itself. To become convinced that you need to be rescued from life's obstacles is never to mature, never to go beyond your acorn stage of development.

A Path to Follow

You can interrupt the control that these destructive elements have over your life by establishing a path, a direction to follow. This program will introduce you to what remains healthy in you, what remains uncontaminated, yearning to progress and mature. You will learn to confront that in you which has become destructive. You will unlearn the patterns of stagnation and replace them with a zest and a spontaneity that have been absent for many years. This program will teach you to "re"-form not only destructive behaviors and tendencies but also your attitude toward life and living.

You will meet such colorful characters as the "Beast," the "Spoiled Child," and the "Insecure Child," who represent aspects of your inner landscape that have become contorted by your addictive behavior. These characters are elements of a technique I have developed in my psychology practice called "Directed Imagination." This is the tool you will use to break the grip of your addiction. Although no two people describe their addictions or habits in exactly the same way, there are universal aspects of addictive behavior that seem to transcend individuality. (For simplicity I will use the term "addictive behavior" to refer to all such behaviors — habits, addictions, phobias, obsessions, and compulsions; distinctions between these various categories will be made when necessary.)

These universal aspects of addictive behavior allow a technique such as Directed Imagination to work just as well for you as it does for someone down the block or across the continent. We are all of the same human fabric and share similar strengths as well as weaknesses. To say that someone has an addiction is no different from saying that human beings are susceptible to getting sore throats. The fact that your throat hurts does not make you a bad person. You are just a bit run-down and your resistance is depleted, leaving you vulnerable to one of those omnipresent viruses that lurk about. The same applies to the human susceptibility to addictive behavior. When overwhelmed or depleted, humans become fertile ground for such psychological "viruses." Just as you would not feel guilty about getting a sore throat, do not berate yourself for your susceptibility to addictive behavior.

In essence, Directed Imagination is a simple, straightforward technique that can transform your addictive experience into more tangible and workable mental images (i.e., the Beast, the Spoiled Child, and the Insecure Child). The healthy part of your mind will use these characterizations to step apart from that in you which has become addicted and contorted. No longer will such contaminating notions as "I can't stop! It's too hard!" spoil your resolve to quit.

Now for the first time you will come to understand that the "I" who cannot stop, who feels it is too hard, is really only one aspect of the self, not in any way representative of the true totality of your being. What has become a fusion (and confusion) of faulty self-perceptions can now be divided into two voices: One voice emanates from what remains healthy in you and the other is addiction's voice of sabotage and seduction. Once this distinction is achieved, once you recognize that your addictive behavior has its own voice separate from your healthy voice, then a sense of legitimate control and optimism can be harnessed.

Letting Go

What exactly happens when you become aware of addictive behavior and decide to break it? Why does it seem impossible just to let it go? Before answering, let me introduce an important concept: the ego. Basically, the ego is that part of you with which you are identified. It is the subjective "I" you refer to whenever you think of yourself. Whenever you define yourself ("I am a teacher" or "I am a nice person"), you are talking about your ego.

For the purpose of Directed Imagination, it is important to understand that your ego becomes defined by that with which you identify. When people contemplate their addictive tendencies, they typically become overwhelmed with thoughts that they are "weak," "sick," or "neurotic." The ego becomes identified with these words and the person feels crushed.

What, on the other hand, would happen if you were able to disengage your identification from that in you which is destructive? What if you were able to step aside and say "That's not what I'm all about. Only a part of me is weak, not all of me!" This is the pulse of Directed Imagination. It allows your ego to gain perspective on itself while simultaneously becoming aware of that part in you which has become destructive. You must never assume that you, your totality, has become negative. Instead you must come to understand that your destructive tendencies are aspects of addiction and habit, not aspects of your ego.

Now apply this understanding to the question of why it seems impossible just to let go of addictive behavior. If you were to say "I can't" break such-and-such habit and believe your words, then the likelihood is small that you would succeed, regardless of the technique or program you employ. If, on the other hand, you come to realize that "I can't" emanates from the voice of addiction and is *not* the voice of your healthy ego, then, and only then, are you in a position to break your habit. You are in this position because you realize that only a part of you "can't." The rest of you, the healthy you, *can*!

No matter how defeated, damaged, or helpless you feel in the face of your addiction, compulsion, phobia, or obsession, you have the strength to stop if you choose to call on it. That strength can be found in the same healthy, adult ego that gets you out of bed every morning and propels you to work, that enables you to fix dinner every night and brush your teeth regularly. This healthy, adult ego is the natural, uncontaminated by-product of learning and maturation. It is a universal propensity for understanding, handling, and surviving your world. Although you may feel psychologically unhealthy, inept, or ineffective, it is, nevertheless, the prodding of your healthy ego that manages life's mundane routines.

It is the distorted thinking perpetuated by the voices of your habit that interferes with your healthy ego responses. Directed Imagination allows you to reconnect with your natural common sense capacity for effective living and to use this ego strength to heal your habit.

You can finally break the psychological grip that has kept you a prisoner to your addiction. Through Directed Imagination, you will be instructed how to confront, discipline, and re-form these voices of rebellion. The leash that has made you an obedient puppy all these years can finally be broken.

The Genesis of This Program

When I first began practicing psychology some years ago, one of the more frequent requests I received from patients was to help them quit smoking. At first my only tool for such a specific request was a working knowledge of hypnosis, which I readily offered. Although hypnosis initially yielded adequate results, relapse remained high. I slowly began to realize that the general addictive experience involved in smoking included much more than simply a compulsion to smoke. It included a very unusual yet unmistakable type of distorted thinking that became particularly evident during the stress of withdrawal (the period immediately following a person's stopping smoking). At this point I had not noticed that this same distorted thinking was also a major component in establishing and maintaining an addiction.

This realization gave birth to Directed Imagination. I began to differentiate the thoughts and perceptions of addiction into three distinct categories, each of which reflects a specific aspect of the addictive struggle: the "Beast," the "Spoiled Child," and the "Insecure Child." The result was a complete approach, capable of covering not only the mechanics of stopping a habit but also the psychology of enduring withdrawal's many distortions.

To my surprise, I found myself using Directed Imagination more and more in my general practice. The material presented in therapy just kept lending itself to this technique. Realizing the potential for Directed Imagination's larger role, I began to refine and customize the technique in order to apply it to a wide range of problems, from weight reduction and other specific requests to more diffuse problems such as anxiety and worry. The results, across the board, were very encouraging. In fact, it was the continual feedback I received on how easy it was to apply Directed Imagination to life situations that encouraged me to consider a self-monitored program, the results of which you now hold in your hands.

1
LOOKING AHEAD:
A Program for Success

Structuring Your Personal Program

What habit do you want to heal? This program can help you win the struggle against a variety of addictions, compulsions, obsessions, and phobias. From the topics below, choose the one that best describes your habit. Follow your specific structural guidelines, found at the beginning of each chapter.

☐ Smoking

Cigarette smoking is the most difficult of all addictions to overcome. I agree wholeheartedly with this bit of current wisdom. But Directed Imagination has worked for many people already, and it will work for you if you follow it to the best of your ability.

Begin by reading Chapter 1 and paying particular attention to the *Steps for Success*.

☐ Compulsive Eating

Directed Imagination can help you deal with any form of compulsive eating — compulsive overeating (you feel driven to binge, your eating is out of control), bulimia (your binges are followed by purges in the form of vomiting, laxatives, or frenetic exercise), anorexia (you starve yourself and/or exercise excessively in an attempt to stay extremely thin), or obsessive food thoughts. However, with some conditions such as anorexia and bulimia, where the underlying dynamics are often deep-seated and resistant to conscious intervention, Directed Imagination should be used in conjunction with psychotherapy or counseling.

Before commencing this program, you should decide on a dietary regime to follow. Although there are an endless number of diets to choose from, select a sensible, nutritious plan that can become more a way of life than just a way of losing weight. You may want to investigate Overeaters Anonymous (a Twelve-Step Program based on the principles of Alcoholics Anonymous), Weight Watchers, or other weight control programs. Making an appointment with a nutritionist would also be helpful. Through an understanding of the Child within, you will finally stop looking for miracles and magic. Once you combine an intelligent way of eating, a philosophy of living life head-on without avoidance, and Directed Imagination, you will be well on your way to a vigorous and healthy life.

Begin to break the compulsive connection by reading Chapter 1 and paying close attention to the *Steps for Success*.

☐ Phobias

Phobias are specific fears that have become connected with a specific person (dentist, doctor, boss, etc.), animals (dogs, bees, spiders, snakes, etc.), objects (needles, knives, guns, etc.), places (open places such as a large stadium or open field; closed places such as a small room, an elevator, or a tunnel; crowded places such as a church or a shopping mall, etc.) or thoughts (fear of flying, driving, drowning, etc.).

The primary difference between a phobia and an obsession is that the phobia is connected exclusively to a fear of something specific. Usually as long as the feared action, place, person, animal, or object is avoided, there is no evident distress. With obsessions, the fears are more diffuse and ruminative. A person with obsessive fears is usually subjected to intrusive thoughts and anxiety wherever she or he is. Directed Imagination can help you break out of the walls created by your fears.

If you want to heal your phobia, read Chapter 1 very carefully. Give special attention to the *Steps for Success*.

☐ Obsessive Thinking

This includes all intrusive thoughts that create anxiety, panic, fear, or worry. Typically, obsessions are rooted in the concept of control. We may ruminate about the loss of control symbolized in such things as illness, failure, accidents, and so on. Included in this category are concerns about jealousy, desire for perfection, and excessive neatness or ambition. Obsessive fears differ from phobic fears in that they are not connected with a specific object, place, or thought.

To begin freeing yourself from obsessive thinking, read Chapter 1 and the *Steps for Success*.

☐ **General Compulsions/Compulsive Gambling**

Compulsive gambling is representative of many compulsions, ordinary activities that have gotten totally out of control. Included in this category are such activities as spending, shopping, nail biting, hoarding, etc. Directed Imagination can be used independently to deal with these compulsions, but if you are dealing with compulsive gambling, this program is enhanced significantly by simultaneous participation in Gamblers Anonymous. There are also groups dealing with spending problems.

Begin to break your compulsion by reading Chapter 1. If you are breaking a gambling compulsion, then Step 3 of the *Steps for Success* is important for you.

☐ **Drug Addiction**

The severe chemical-psychological dependence created by drug abuse makes withdrawal particularly difficult. Directed Imagination is a helpful tool, but as with any method, there are limitations. With alcoholism and severe drug dependence, both of which have such profound and far-reaching implications both physically and psychologically, a purely self-monitored program is just not enough. In these particular addictions, denial is a very strong defense that limits your capacity for consciousness.

This being the case, a more practical approach is found in such programs as Alcoholics Anonymous or Narcotics Anonymous, which, in addition to a well-structured Twelve-Step approach, heavily emphasize the social or group aspect of the treatment. For someone prone to severe denial, this social component provides a very potent means of both objective feedback and emotional support. I would recommend Directed Imagination as an adjunct to either of these or similar programs. People I have worked with in both A.A. and N.A. feel that Directed Imagination is completely compatible with their program and their sobriety.

You can begin to deal with your drug addiction by reading Chapter 1 and implementing the *Steps for Success*, especially Step 3.

☐ **Alcohol Addiction**

The previous remarks about drug addiction certainly apply here as well. Since denial is such an integral part of substance addictions and the social component so useful in recovery, I would strongly recommend that Directed Imagination be used in conjunction with participation in Alcoholics Anonymous.

Read Chapter 1, paying close attention to the *Steps for Success*. Begin to implement Step 3.

Directed Imagination is a technique that has evolved into a broad-based program for gaining control over most problems stemming from habit and addiction. Regardless of whether you are quitting smoking, trying to lose weight, dealing with phobic thoughts, or trying to break a compulsive ritual, the application of Directed Imagination remains virtually the same in each case. Yet each problem does require emphasizing different components of the program (e.g., hypnosis, diet, journal, etc.). Because of this variation in emphasis, different structural elements are recommended for each addictive category. We are not referring to different techniques, however, just different emphases within the same method.

Specifically, the program encompasses the following key aspects: Directed Imagination, attitudinal preparation, physical preparation, environmental or external preparation, hypnosis, a journal, and establishing a psychological context. Each of these concepts is developed fully in succeeding chapters. Read the chapters sequentially, allowing yourself to build a progressive understanding of your responsibilities in habit re-formation.

A mistake often made by other approaches or methods is to focus too heavily on only one or two of these components, allowing the neglected aspect(s) to find the back door and sabotage your efforts. It is like spending thousands of dollars to decorate a house, never realizing that the structural supports are being insidiously gnawed away by termites in the basement. You do not have to be aware of termites to have your house collapse — unconsciousness in any pursuit invites disaster!

Structuring for Success

A word I use to describe the preparations required in this program is "structuring," which refers to what you will be doing to your thinking, your attitudes, and your world in order to become ready for any contingency. "Structuring" describes the implementation of various techniques and strategies designed to bolster, compensate, or otherwise fill in any gaps that may exist in your character. These gaps represent vulnerabilities, chinks in the armor, where your strength and conviction alone cannot be relied upon to overcome your addiction.

Think of these structural supports as spokes on a bicycle wheel. When all, or even most, of a wheel's spokes are added to the outer rim, the result is an astoundingly rigid and durable product. Each of the elements introduced in this program provides a kind of spoke. When combined, they offer you the same kind of structural rigidity and resilience inherent in a bicycle wheel. Just as the wheel absorbs the bumps and lumps of a ride, your structural preparations will allow you to roll through the unknown terrain of the withdrawal experience with confidence.

Structuring provides a "braced" attitude, without which you become easy prey to withdrawal's confused thoughts and deceptions. Imagine yourself riding along in a car. Another car runs a stop sign right in front of you. In the second before your foot reaches the brake, your whole body begins to react. Your hands tighten around the wheel. Your body begins to pump adrenalin. Your respiration increases. Your muscles begin to anticipate the possible impact. In a word, you become braced for a collision. Being braced is an anticipatory readiness for danger and includes a psychological as well as a physical dimension.

When you come face to face with the myriad withdrawal symptoms typical of habit re-formation, you will be in a much better position if you can get braced before you collide. This can only be accomplished through diligent structural preparation. In a now-famous study, three groups of volunteers were injected with adrenalin. One group was given accurate information as to what changes to expect (e.g., increased heart rate, respiration, etc.). A second group was given inaccurate information. A third group was given no information. The results showed that the group given accurate information (i.e., information that adequately explained their psychological and physical experiences) reported the least amount of discomfort. Those misinformed actually experienced more distress than the uninformed group. This study clearly illustrates the need to accurately anticipate both the physical (if you are dealing with substance withdrawal) and psychological components of habit re-formation.

This capacity for anticipation, paired with a restructuring of your attitudes, can be used to help you become psychologically more grounded. Having each foot firmly planted on solid ground prevents the head from floating up into hysterical speculations that, if left unchallenged, will send you clamoring back to the security of your habit. When you are going through withdrawal, it does not take much to disorient you. I recall a frantic call from one patient who had just quit smoking the night before. He wanted to know what life could possibly offer him now that smoking was gone. He was not speaking rhetorically, nor was he suicidal. He just could not comprehend a life without his little companions.

It is your structural foundation of Directed Imagination and mental preparedness that will sustain you through these malicious thoughts. Especially during those first few days, you may become too agitated even to want to think, much less read or listen to a tape. This is when you will want to have in place a sturdy structure that will maintain your balance in spite of the confusion going on in your head. The more automatic your responses, the less your danger. This reflexive reaction is your best insurance that you will get through the ordeal in spite of any and all chaos you may encounter. Spend the time to establish these reflexes. Be thorough. You will not regret it.

What to Expect

Starting with **CHAPTER 2**, you will be introduced to Directed Imagination with its characterizations: the Beast, the Spoiled Child, and the Insecure Child. Through discussion and case example you will see how these mental images of your addiction are capable of restructuring your attitudes, your thoughts, and your perceptions during your struggle to heal your habit.

CHAPTER 3 will address the actual nuts and bolts involved in getting your inner, as well as your outer, environment ready. The major thrust of this chapter is to provide you with a regime of rest, exercise, and diet capable of reducing anxiety and tension naturally. Certain foods, for example, when eaten regularly can produce the brain chemicals responsible for relaxation. Just as one food can foster relaxation, another can inhibit this response. Chapter 3 will acquaint you with rest, exercise, and nutritional information that will be invaluable in dealing not only with the pangs of withdrawal but also with the increased tension and anxiety created by the process of habit re-formation.

CHAPTER 4 will introduce you to the mechanics of keeping a journal. Habit re-formation typically brings forward an abundance of thoughts, feelings, and reactions, all competing for conscious attention. Maintaining focus while sifting through this cornucopia of experience is the essential reason I have included a journal in the program. Not only will keeping a journal assist you in identifying the characters of Directed Imagination more easily, a careful rereading of your entries will make various addictive trends and themes more apparent.

An equally important advantage in keeping a journal is the feedback you are able to obtain. You can use this feedback, this "mirroring" of your behavior or thoughts, to shape your future responses. From this feedback, for example, you will quickly find out whether eating a preventive snack or walking the dog brings you the most relief from withdrawal. Likewise, you will learn which behaviors are taboo and need to be avoided at all costs. If, for example, you are trying to lose weight and control an eating compulsion, you may need to find a new route home from work, one that does not go past a string of fast-food restaurants with their alluring drive-in windows. You will be absolutely amazed at how the most obvious facts, if left only to mental recollection, can be forgotten during the throes of withdrawal. The journal will compensate for this understandable weakness of focus.

CHAPTER 5 deals with the mechanics of hypnosis: what it is and what it is not. You will be instructed specifically how to make an appropriate hypnosis tape for your particular problem.* The hypnotic experience represents a strong element in your structure.

Human nature being what it is, we are all too inclined to look for free lunches, to avoid pain, and to seek pleasure. Many people approach hypnosis as something rather mystical, where their minds will be controlled without any effort or difficulty — abracadabra! Like most people, your image of hypnosis was probably shaped by Hollywood's or television's portrayal of the hypnotist with penetrating dark eyes and

---

* Although complete instructions for making your own hypnosis tape are found in Chapter 5, a high-quality hypnosis tape *Healing Your Habits*, narrated by Dr. Luciani, is available from LuraMedia, Post Office Box 261668, San Diego, CA 92126.

perfunctory goatee, swinging a gold pocket watch while lulling his patient to sleep.

Clinical hypnosis has absolutely nothing to do with these popular theatrical notions. For the purpose of habit re-formation, hypnosis is basically an experience of deep relaxation and concentrated focus, one not easily achieved through normal consciousness. Within this state of hyperfocus, positive suggestions are thoroughly and completely absorbed. Most people find hypnosis of this type to be a very enjoyable and restful experience.

CHAPTER 6 will introduce you to the psychological context, which represents the final stage of your program. Establishing the psychological context is essential if you plan to avoid either an eventual relapse or a habit substitution (e.g., giving up marijuana and switching to alcohol). The psychological context brings you to an elemental understanding of your addiction. From this vantage point your Directed Imagination becomes an unassailable weapon against addiction.

This, then, is a prelude to what is ahead. Think of the preliminary structural elements of the program as your preparatory stretching. Just as a well-seasoned athlete comes to appreciate the necessity for proper preparation and would never risk injury by skimping on her or his limbering up, you must respect your need for psychological stretching as you diligently follow the structural preparations presented in this book. Chapter by chapter you will begin to stretch the necessary muscles that will be called upon to perform when you decide to reclaim your life.

The chapters of this book are meant to be read sequentially. The *Steps for Success* at the end of each chapter will assist you in focusing your attention on what is essential. Only after reading through the book and completing your *Checklist* at the end of Chapter 5 should you plan your "cessation date," the moment when you actually stop your addiction.

You will find that most of the structural elements in the program are rather straightforward, requiring little if any rehearsal or practice to implement. The only exception is Directed Imagination, which you will need to become familiar with before initiating your moment of liberation. This familiarization need not be arduous or time-consuming. All you need to do is acquaint yourself with the basic concept of these inner characters and then go on with your day, casually looking for examples in your own behavior and thoughts. It is not really as difficult as it may first appear. These characters are downright obvious once you know what to look for. Believe me, once you start hunting for that Spoiled Child, Insecure Child, or Beast, you will not have far to look.

This preparatory work with Directed Imagination is essential because once you stop your addiction, withdrawal will make it very difficult to concentrate on learning anything new. (Note: Although the term "withdrawal" is usually associated with substance addiction, for the sake of simplicity I will use the term to refer to life without your habit, whatever it is.) Being able to apply Directed Imagination before you quit assures that you can keep a grip on your intentions when withdrawal begins.

Once you have stopped your addictive behavior, you will be involved in withdrawal. This, of course, is the critical phase of habit reformation. During withdrawal you will want to have in place all the structural elements of the program to insure that you possess the necessary reflexes to act appropriately. The less you leave to chance, or to your ability to think, the better. In time, your Directed Imagination will establish the upper hand over the chaos, and you will begin to experience complete control and confidence.

It is precisely because of this anticipated chaos that thoroughness is essential throughout each facet of the program. You cannot possibly know ahead of time what will be a critical asset when things do get rough. Be safe. Resist any temptation to delete material or to find shortcuts. Just make yourself follow the program with all the patience and perseverance you can muster.

Preparing to Stop

There is no specific time line for learning and implementing this material. Generally, I would suggest that you give yourself about one week to read and practice Chapter 2 on Directed Imagination and about another week to read Chapters 3, 4, 5, and 6 and to implement the *Steps for Success* in Chapters 3, 4, and 5. This will require some physical preparations (e.g., making a hypnosis tape, setting up a journal, food shopping) along with some psychological groundwork. By the end of two weeks, using your *Checklist* at the end of Chapter 5 for a guide, you should be ready to stop your addiction.

Remember, these are just general guidelines. If you feel you need more time, then by all means please allow it. These habits took more than a day to establish, and they will take more than a day to extinguish. If, on the other hand, you want to compress the program into less than two weeks, be very careful. Your exuberance may in fact be a disguised form of sabotage. You may end up running around after one day's effort saying, "See, I knew it. It was just too hard. Nothing works for me!" If you feel it is absolutely necessary to stop your addictive behavior in less than two weeks, then at least put most of your efforts and emphasis into developing your skill with Directed Imagination. Enthusiasm is great, but impulsiveness can lead to an incomplete foundation and failure.

With certain addictive behaviors such as obsessions, phobias, ruminative fears or worries, there is no specific moment of habit cessation. Rather than a planned moment of cessation, you will experience a gradual process of cessation. Using the program as outlined for obsessions or phobias, you will begin to gradually diminish these fears until you reach a point where they cease to bother you.

I realize that for some, especially for those whose obsession involves a great deal of control, the words "gradually diminish" may actually increase your anxiety. If you are of this frame of mind and need a more definite handle, then go ahead and select a specific time and date. You can use your hypnosis tape as a planned point of cessation. Just read through the chapters, casually preparing yourself. Then on your planned night of cessation, listen to your tape. From this point on, try to maintain a complete commitment to the program.

For those of you planning to give up a substance (such as nicotine, caffeine, or sugar) or a habit (such as gambling or shopping), arranging your cessation around a predetermined block of time will give you a distinct advantage: You will be able to pre-arrange your environment, your commitments, and your duties in such a way as to free the maximum psychic energy. When, for example, I discuss smoke cessation with a client in my practice, I suggest that he or she begin on Thursday night and keep Friday, Saturday, and Sunday as free as possible. If you are like most people, this will mean taking a day off work or, if you have children, arranging for your spouse or family to take complete charge of them.

If you happen to be a bit compulsive, you are probably cringing over this last statement, feeling that you must be in charge of all worldly events at all times. No one is saying you cannot, or could not, juggle your normal life and quit your habit at the same time. It just makes a lot more sense to conserve all your energy for the momentous task ahead. If, in the normal course of a day, you expend a certain amount of effort handling the demands and pressures of your job or the stress involved in keeping your children from combat, then you realize that there is a psychological price to pay. Since you have only a finite amount of psychic energy available on any given day, when you go beyond this limit, you become tired and burned out. You may be able to call upon your reserves, but once the well runs dry, you lose not only the ability to handle even minor disturbances but also the capacity to endure the tumult of withdrawal.

In order to avoid such depletion, you must respect life's limitations. Remember, it is up to you to actively arrange for a hassle-free environment ahead of time. Do not be naive about your responsibilities. All efforts to give yourself every advantage at this point make good sense. This is not a good time to hope you get lucky.

If you are dealing with substance addiction, you will want to start letting people know about your decision to quit. By broadcasting your intentions, you build a constructive anxiety about the whole process, a form of accountability that adds a very potent incentive. It is a lot easier to lose face with yourself than to lose face with your friends. Both are humiliating experiences, to be sure, but if push comes to shove, you are more likely to avoid social embarrassment. It is always possible to rationalize personal embarrassment. Social accountability represents just one more thread you should attempt to weave into the fabric of your cessation program.

If, on the other hand, you are dealing with a thought disorder, such as an obsession or a phobia, unless people already know about your difficulty, I would not suggest informing them at this time. Typically, insecurity is a major component in these problems. You do not need to develop any paranoia about what people are thinking about you or your problem. You do not need to feel any additional anxiety.

Whether you choose to go it alone or with a loved one depends on how you have performed in the past during adversity. Are you the type who is more sick when someone is around to lean on, or do you truly benefit from the support (and distraction) of a companion? If you feel you are the latter type, then please, have your "significant other" become familiar with this program prior to your target date. This is an important point. Even a potentially helpful person can turn out to be a real burden if he or she has a distorted perception of what you will be going through. Such a helper, witnessing your struggle, may wind up in a frenzied panic — at which point, all efforts at helping shift from blessing to burden. You do not need to be rescued. You need to be encouraged, supported, and loved.

Make sure you forewarn your beloved support team to take nothing you say or do personally. When the Beast begins to dance on your nerves, you are likely to displace some of your irritation on anyone who happens to be within reach at the moment. If you have done your Directed Imagination homework in Chapter 2, you will find that you can keep most of your frustrations focused on the Beast, Spoiled Child, or Insecure Child, thus avoiding a good deal of this lashing out. But, alas, regardless of how expert you get with your Directed Imagination, you are just not going to feel as composed and loving as Mother Theresa during this period.

Remember Murphy's third law: "If anything can possibly go wrong, it will." His rarely quoted first law also applies to healing your habits: "Nothing is as easy as it looks." The less you leave to chance, the better off you will be. Put away your Wonder Woman or Superman cape. Begin to develop a comprehensive and realistic approach to your goal. Such an approach will maximize every possibility for success.

Make up your mind that this will be the first and last time you will ever have to go through this ordeal. If this is not your first time, then, for goodness' sake, make it your last!

C-Day

Thursday night, your cessation date, arrives. You begin by listening to the hypnosis tape you have prepared. An hour or so later is bedtime. By Friday morning you will have already put eleven or twelve hours of withdrawal behind you. By Sunday morning, many of the toxins — both physical and psychological — will be flushed from your body! Of course, the precise pace of your withdrawal will be determined by your own unique physiology and your own psychological reactions to these experiences. But by the time the Sunday morning paper arrives, you will have perhaps the most difficult and dangerous period of quitting behind you.

As we said before, those of you who want to break an addiction to alcohol or drugs will find this program most helpful in conjunction with participation in Alcoholics Anonymous or Narcotics Anonymous. You might want to begin by listening to your hypnosis tape and then attending an A.A. or N.A. meeting. Supplement frequent meetings and the Twelve-Step Program with Directed Imagination, rest, exercise, diet, journaling, and your hypnosis tape.

As you begin to work out the necessary logistics for these initial days of withdrawal, remind yourself that this is going to be the most important, life-saving weekend of your life. Do not cut corners! Build up to your weekend gradually. Keep your spouse, baby-sitters, family, and friends apprised of their roles in your game plan. If ever there was a time to pool all your resources, this is it! Do not be afraid to ask for favors. Once you explain your unique needs for this very significant weekend, you will be surprised how many will rally behind you.

As the Chinese philosopher Lao-tse once said: "A journey of a thousand miles must begin with a single step." Concern yourself only with each individual step, one at a time. Whatever gets thrown at you during your habit re-formation experience, just stay in the moment. Fight only the battle at hand before looking ahead. There will always be a temptation to leap into the future with feelings of "How will I go on? I can't do this for one more day!" If you get seduced by this whining, then in no time at all you will be experiencing the hysteria and panic that defeats so many. If instead you confine your focus to your immediate path, forgetting the battles of tomorrow or next week, you will always be in a position to manage what gets thrown at you. This journey, any journey, is accomplished by a succession of incremental steps, one, by one, by one.

Steps For Success

1 If you are dealing with a substance addiction, it is time to broadcast your intentions about quitting. Share the news with some significant and caring people in your life. If, on the other hand, you are dealing with thoughts (e.g., obsessions, worries, phobias, etc.), you should share your intentions only with the most intimate people in your life who are already aware of your difficulties.

2 This is a good time to take a piece of paper and jot down *at least* five reasons why you have elected to quit your habit. Keep your list handy, in your wallet or purse. You may need an occasional reminder when withdrawal's clouds of deception distort your perceptions.

3 If you are battling a substance addiction such as drug addiction, alcohol addiction, or compulsive overeating, now is the time to scout out such groups as Alcoholics Anonymous, Narcotics Anonymous, or Overeaters Anonymous. Compulsive gamblers should check to see if your city has a Gamblers Anonymous group. City or county mental health offices can usually provide information on such groups if they are not listed in the telephone book. Support groups may be available to help you deal with your habit. Check it out. Call to find out meeting times. Arrange to go to a meeting with a friend.

2
RECOGNIZING THE CHARACTERS OF YOUR HABIT:
Directed Imagination

Structuring Your Personal Program

☐ **Smoking**
Read Chapter 2 in its entirety. Pay particular attention to the Beast and to Don's journal. Special emphasis should be given to the *Steps for Success*.

☐ **Compulsive Eating**
Read all of Chapter 2. Fred's story illustrates how Directed Imagination can deal with compulsive eating. With an eating compulsion it is likely that you will encounter all three characters: the Beast, the Spoiled Child, and the Insecure Child. Special attention should be given to the *Steps for Success*.

☐ **Phobias**
Read all of Chapter 2 with the exception of "The Beast" (this section applies only to substance addictions). Special emphasis should be given to the *Steps for Success* (omit Step 3.C).

☐ **Obsessive Thinking**
Read Chapter 2 carefully. Mary's story is an example of obsessive thinking. You may omit the section on "The Beast" (this applies only to substance addictions). The *Steps for Success* are of particular importance to you (omit Step 3.C on the Beast).

Lowering anxiety is your first objective when dealing with an attack of obsessive thinking. The irony is that most people inadvertently wind up doing exactly the opposite. What happens is that the anxiety causes panic, which creates the reaction: "I have to stop this anxiety. I can't let this continue. I have to stop it!" By demanding to control the anxiety, you actually wind up increasing it. In a sense, you become anxious about being anxious — the proverbial dog chasing its tail!

A much better philosophy is to learn how to ride out these anxiety attacks. The quickest way not to get overwhelmed by anxiety is to try to accept, rather than avoid, the anxiety. Although this may sound a bit contradictory at first, I assure you, if you are trying compulsively to control anxiety, you are probably suffering needlessly.

Begin to develop a more casual attitude toward the anxiety itself: "Okay, it's got me again. How can I hold on until it lets me go?" This attitude will eventually teach you one of the most important lessons in habit re-formation: to relinquish your controlling grip on life and to let go! In the section on "The Spoiled Child," the comments about tantrums will be helpful.

☐ **General Compulsions/Compulsive Gambling**
Read Chapter 2, skipping the section on "The Beast" (this section applies only to substance addictions). Sam's story offers an example of applying Directed Imagination to a gambling compulsion. Special emphasis should be given to the *Steps for Success* (you may omit Step 3.C).

☐ **Drug Addiction**
Read Chapter 2. Pay particular attention to "The Beast." The *Steps for Success* can help you break your addiction.

☐ **Alcohol Addiction**
Read Chapter 2. Pay particular attention to "The Beast." Special emphasis should be given to the *Steps for Success*.

Imagine, for a moment, that you are taking a plane ride to some far-off place. You find your way to your seat and settle in. A few minutes later another passenger arrives and occupies the seat next to you. With a pleasant smile she introduces herself as Kathy.

Your first impression is of an energetic, self-confident person. Her appearance is neat and fashionable, with obvious attention to detail. She appears to be a person who has it all together. As the plane taxis, you begin to relax and settle into casual conversation. She makes small talk look like an art as she amusingly quips about airport experiences she has had. Time passes quickly as you find Kathy's company thoroughly enjoyable and entertaining.

After absentmindedly glancing out the window for what seems to be only a moment, you realize that Kathy has become quiet. Looking back at her, you are quite startled. Her face has changed; she looks pale, sickly. As she stares blankly ahead, you notice her hands folding and unfolding nervously. She leans forward in her seat, as if confused about getting up or staying seated. She turns toward you, and immediately you sense a kind of tension and urgency in what she is about to say. She begins to speak; her voice is different, somewhat higher, less controlled.

She tells you that flying is very difficult for her. What follows are words of panic, fear, and helplessness: "I can't stand this! I'm really scared. I can't breathe. I feel like I'm going to suffocate." You nervously listen for a while, trying to figure out how you can offer some help, some comfort, something! You begin by trying to calm her down, encouraging her to talk about her job, anything to get her mind off her fears.

She pauses only for a brief second and then begins to ruminate again, as if you had not said a word. Her breathing becomes more shallow and rapid, her thoughts more chaotic and panicky. By this time you, of course, are feeling powerless and frightened. Kathy is obviously caught in the grip of something far beyond your ability to understand, much less to control. What can it be that takes such a seemingly relaxed, together woman and reduces her to such a panicked child?

Kathy's mind, at some critical point, was taken over by a less rational, insecure kind of voice that began to fill her with an avalanche of claustrophobic thoughts. Once these thoughts began to cascade into her head, she was lost, no longer able to control her thinking. Where does this less rational voice come from? Why could Kathy not decide to ignore the voice, to calm herself?

You might ask yourself the same questions: Why have you become a victim of addictive behavior? What voice rules you?

Three Voices of Addiction

In helping people work through their addictions, I have discovered three characterizations, or mental images, that represent addictive or destructive thinking. I am not, of course, referring to actual voices. What I am trying to describe is an experience where what goes through your mind is very different from your usual, everyday thinking process. Ideas and concepts not in tune with your rational wishes take over. Sometimes this takeover is a gradual escalating process. At other times, as with Kathy, the thoughts go from light to dark in a matter of minutes, if not seconds.

Kathy's normal, appropriate thinking was taken over by an intrusive, frightened type of thinking, thoughts that convinced her that some aspect of life had to be avoided (e.g., being confined in a plane). Based on these thoughts and perceptions of insecurity, a sense of panic was generated. I call this the experience of the "Insecure Child." It represents a specific way of thinking capable of turning your world upside down. From this perspective, nothing can be trusted.

Using Directed Imagination, you will learn to reach out and connect with the Insecure Child. You will develop a more complete self-awareness that will allow you to nurture the Child and calm his or her panic. The habits and addictions, the destructive thinking, and the self-sabotage will finally be interrupted, as the Insecure Child is encouraged to risk trusting life once again (or perhaps for the first time).

A second character and close cousin to the Insecure Child is the Spoiled Child. Like the Insecure Child, the Spoiled Child represents a regressive inability to accept or deal with some aspect of life. The Insecure Child's strength lies in the ability to create fear and panic. The Spoiled Child's speciality is manipulation. The Spoiled Child is experienced as a destructive or abusive pattern of thinking that can coerce or intimidate you into continuing your habit.

Depending on your unique disposition, you will find that one or both of these "Children" are integral aspects of all your addictive behavior. Whenever your ego becomes compromised by an addiction or habit, it is these characters that become the mental manipulators and, at times, the tormentors of your life. They are adept at intimidating or panicking whatever remains healthy in you. Once manipulated, your tendency is to become overwhelmed. When this happens, you either give up or give in to your destructive patterns. Then, like Kathy, every thought gets prefaced with the words "I can't."

One last character I call the "Beast." The Beast is the voice of cravings. Unless your addictive problem will entail withdrawal from a specific substance, you will not get to meet this unsavory character. In essence, the Beast is synonymous with craving. It is the mental image of the physical discomfort you experience when you stop taking into your body a substance to which your body is accustomed. Although the Beast is prominently displayed in such addictions as alcohol, nicotine, cocaine, caffeine, and the like, you may also meet this completely loathsome character in food-related obsessions and compulsions.

Some confusion can arise here because both the Spoiled Child and the Insecure Child are quite capable of very Beast-like behavior. For the purpose of habit re-formation, all you need to know is whether or not your withdrawal is from an addictive substance. If such a substance is involved, you will meet the Beast. If you are not dealing with physical detoxification, then it is the Beast-like qualities of either the Spoiled or the Insecure Child that will torment you.

A friend of mine was compulsively involved in running — about seventy-five miles per week. He suffered a knee injury and was quickly introduced to the Beast-like capacity of his Spoiled Child. For more than a week he hobbled around, biting everyone's head off, constantly bemoaning his fate ("It's just not fair!"). I suggested that he try swimming until his leg healed. He actually got red in the face as he told me I just did not understand. The Spoiled Child often feels misunderstood.

As science probes further and further into the chemistry of habit and addiction, it would not surprise me if scientists were to find that certain brain chemicals released during running are actually addictive. Research is already suggesting that certain food sugars and fats can have some of the same addictive characteristics as a drug. We are getting an ever clearer picture of the essence and substance of addiction.

For now, however, you can work with the distinction of Beast versus Beast-like Child reactions to your addiction. If, however, you feel intuitively certain that whatever it is you are withdrawing from has a chemically addictive component, then by all means use the Beast as your antagonist whenever you encounter your cravings.

Differentiating each character is important because each requires a slightly different response from you. The Beast, for example, needs to be tamed. The Beast acts instinctively. Like an animal, it seeks its cravings. You do not need to negotiate with it; you just need to domesticate it.

Imagine picking up a stray dog. At first you need to be very careful, very leery of its wild nature. You could very well get nipped. You need to take a methodical approach, gradually shaping what you deem to be appropriate behavior for the dog and sternly discouraging what you view as inappropriate. If you are patient, firm, persistent, and encouraging, you will train the dog to yield to your intentions. Once the dog submits to your authority, you can live together in perfect harmony. But do not be fooled: Regardless of how well-trained, given the right circumstances, any dog is capable of reverting to its wild nature. By keeping the upper hand and respecting the nature of the beast, you can realistically minimize, if not eliminate, the possibility of being bitten. You can tame your Beast, but, considering its fundamental nature, you will probably never be able to indulge in your addictive substance again. Or as they say in Alcoholics Anonymous: "Once an alcoholic, always an alcoholic."

The Spoiled Child, on the other hand, does not need to be tamed. It needs to be guided by mature, adult strength. The Spoiled Child does what it does because it has come to realize power in your weakness. Once you begin to allow this Child to experience your resolve and your clarity of conviction, then it will begin to realize that the only advantage is to go along with you. Going against you no longer intimidates you. You ignore its tantrums and encourage positive, mature thinking.

The Insecure Child, more than the Spoiled Child, needs support and encouragement. The major difference is that the Spoiled Child tries to defy, while the Insecure Child tries to defend itself against life. For the Insecure Child you need to build a trust in your mature capacity to take charge. Through effective and courageous acceptance of life, you begin to send new messages to this Child. Once the Insecure Child becomes convinced that you can handle things, it can begin to grow toward rather than away from life.

All three characters represent arrested potential. At first you will be instructed to sort out their voices and distinguish them from the voice of your mature ego. This will give you a clearer perspective on and understanding of the patterns of your habit. Eventually, when these characters surrender to your intentions, you will have inherited their energy. The tamed Beast will offer vitality and ambition. The Children, as they grow and mature, will offer a capacity for expansion and personal development. What has been frozen in you will begin to thaw. The squandered efforts of your habit will become available in the form of useful energy for effective living.

When you are dealing with a substance addiction, all three characters may be deployed against you. They may, in fact, take turns working you over. On the other hand, in thought disorders such as obsessions, phobias, and compulsions (where no dependency exists on a particular addictive substance), you will be spared a confrontation with the Beast. You will not, unfortunately, escape the Spoiled or the Insecure Child.

What you will learn in this chapter is the capacity to recognize the characterizations of your specific addictive habit. You will first delineate, moment by moment, exactly who is doing your thinking. Then you will be ready to start an internal dialogue and, if need be, a confrontation with your tormentors. From this dialogue will come the ability to reassert your mature, healthy ego and to demand your life back.

Directed Imagination is a technique designed to realign your thinking, a good portion of which has been made unconscious by your addictive habits. Whether you look inside and find the Beast, the Spoiled Child, or the Insecure Child, your work remains the same: to identify your regressive or destructive thinking and then to clothe these thoughts with the appropriate characterization. Once dressed in these colorful mental images, the chaotic and confused thoughts of your addictive behavior will acquire a personality. At this point their destructive intentions will become exposed to the full light of the conscious ego. Once they are revealed, you can make a choice based on your healthy desires, a choice to finally stop being a spectator to your own destructive habits, to become an active participant in life.

Begin by reading through the personifications outlined. Ultimately, it will be your job to select the character that best describes your addictive difficulty at any given moment. At times the Beast will rear its ugly head and demand brutal compliance. At other times your feelings will be more like a pathetic or manipulative Child trying to sabotage your efforts. You will be surprised at how clear these patterns become once you begin to own up to your habit and listen to its voices.

The Insecure Child

The Insecure Child aspect of addiction is typified by fear and distrust. Imagine a young child who has become very frightened and distrustful, a child who is forever anticipating all that can go wrong with life. When this attitude persists into adulthood, you perceive life as a dangerous and forbidding place. You find yourself living in a chronic state of dread. Your feelings can range from simple obsessive worry about how your hair looks to a full-fledged panic attack about getting stuck in traffic. The Insecure Child looks at life not as a glass that is half full or half empty but as a glass about to break! Life is all gloom and doom. This Child is a scaredy-cat who is never a match for this frightening world. Everything and everyone is seen as having the potential to turn on this Child and take away the precious little security he or she has.

Before you get defensive and insist, "Oh no, I'm an upbeat person. I'm no scaredy-cat!" remember that the Insecure Child is capable of sabotaging your genuinely healthy nature. Like Kathy in the initial example, what is left after your mind has become corrupted is a distortion, a pathetic shred of your true character. Perhaps you have never noticed how much you change when you become this Child, but starting now you must begin to carefully observe these transformations.

Not everyone has the dubious honor of having a resident Insecure Child. What circumstances lead to such a troublesome development? How does one come by such a fragile disposition? The Insecure Child originates in your early developmental experiences. Think of your life as a house with a mouse. As beautiful and solid as your home may be, one small crack is all that a little fieldmouse needs to enter. Once inside, the little critters have a way of multiplying at an astonishing rate. Your wounds from the past are the crack in the foundation. From this entry point the Insecure Child is able to enter and scurry through your healthy house.

Your sense of security depends on whether your developing ego had the opportunity to experience, and feel embraced by, a competent, loving adult. Such an adult would have allowed you to be carefree and unconcerned with anything beyond your own natural development. When a child grows up in such an atmosphere, anxiety and insecurity are reduced, if not eliminated. If, on the other hand, you were brought up with inconsistency, conflict, or abuse, then insecurity probably flourished.

Even if you did not have an alcoholic or abusive parent, you may have developed a wounded sense of security. Take, for example, the parent who, out of "love," never stops taking care of the child, who is always protecting, giving, sheltering. This child may grow up without learning to handle life. He or she may learn only how to remain a child. This unique type of insecurity can leave an adult fearful of life's responsibilities. Such adults expect to be taken care of and become absolutely hysterical at the notion of being alone. Thus the Insecure Child is primarily a manifestation of a child who became fearful of some aspect of life.

All security begins with love. Sounds so simple, does it not? When love is inconsistent, overbearing, or absent, the child becomes more and more compulsive about finding security. Take, for example, a child who has found that accomplishment buys the attention of an alcoholic or unloving parent. This might sow the seeds for perfectionistic, obsessive struggles that would only intensify with age.

Although many different scenarios of childhood woundedness could be presented here, the end result remains the same: an Insecure Child who grows up seeking security in a world that he or she has come to distrust. A good illustration of this is the credit-card junkie who compulsively buys things in order to feel good. Whether it is buying shoes or books, cars or clothes, this compulsion offers the compensatory feeling of being appreciated and rewarded. First there is an experience of exhilaration, a high, while shopping. When the shoes come home, however, and join an army of other shoes crammed into the closet, reality gives way to depression as the insecure person realizes that nothing has really changed. The emptiness goes on. Addictive habits are the parasites of this wound called insecurity.

The Insecure Child is fundamentally the voice of distrust. Key in on this concept. It is this distrust, this wariness and suspicion of life, that winds up instigating a particular protective reaction. Unfortunately in you this protective reaction has taken the form of an addiction or obsession.

Distrust can be projected onto your body, leading to fears of physical vulnerability (e.g., fears of illness, dying, accidents). If the distrust is projected onto your relationships, you may develop a fear of abandonment. This particular fear may prod you into compulsive pursuits: "If I can just accomplish that, then I will be loved." Perfectionism and related compulsions all fall into this category.

Sometimes this distrust is projected onto fate. Fear of accidents and various phobias become expressions of this profound doubt about the continuity of life. Distrust can become superstitious, leading to various compulsive rituals intended to control fate. I recall a man who felt that if he did not check his stove over and over again (sometimes going back to the house more than ten times after he had driven away), his house would burn down.

All of the above originated in some early woundedness that has been projected onto some aspect of life. Once this projection takes place, you become a pawn in an addictive or obsessive struggle that grips you from the depths of your unconscious. Through the concept of the Insecure Child, you can confront that which has become so distorted and so distrustful in yourself. For the first time you will begin to heal the wounds that have festered all these years. Once the Insecure Child is challenged with a healthy, adult perspective on life, she or he can start to build trust in your resources. You need to convince the Insecure Child that life can be worthwhile, if not wonderful.

■ MARY

Let me give a brief example of the Insecure Child. Mary is a middle-aged woman, married, with two adolescent children. She is employed as a computer programmer. She originally came into therapy because of the tremendous guilt and depression she felt over her infatuation with a man she met in her karate class. Mary's case, a somewhat common midlife dilemma, is very indicative of what happens when insecurity resurfaces and gets projected onto someone other than one's spouse. Mary had become completely obsessed with this other man, so much so that her job, marriage, and friendships were all jeopardized. Here is her journal account:

> *JANUARY 28: Saw Ron* [the man at karate class] *tonight. I can only describe it as physical pain. . . . only want to be with him.*
>
> *FEBRUARY 1: I've been trying to use the concept of the Insecure Child, but it's like I really don't want to spoil what I feel for Ron. I don't want to do anything that could jeopardize such a beautiful feeling. . . . I need him so much!*
>
> *FEBRUARY 5: I was reading my last entry and realized that it was probably my Insecure Child writing those words. Do "I" really need him, or is it the Insecure Child who does? I'm going to call the Insecure Child "Scared Mary."*
>
> *FEBRUARY 8: Scared Mary says that Ron would know how to treat me . . . not like Tom* [her husband]. *I asked Scared Mary why Ron was so perfect, so wonderful . . . no answer.*
>
> *FEBRUARY 13: Bad day. I just couldn't get out of bed. I don't want to live my life without Ron. . . . Should I tell Tom? What will the kids think? . . . Help! I can't do anything except think of Ron. I feel so empty.*
>
> *FEBRUARY 15: Talked with Scared Mary today. She was feeling desperate again. She wants me to leave home and tell Ron about my feelings for him! I finally managed to take a stand against Scared Mary. I told her to cool it. No one is leaving home. I actually began to feel a little better.*
>
> *FEBRUARY 16: Can't stop thinking about Ron — what else is new? Feel like I'm going crazy. Wait a second, let me correct that: I'm not going crazy; Scared Mary is going crazy! That's it! Scared Mary can't live without Ron — I can! Saying it that way really helps. . . . Scared Mary wants to indulge in these romantic fantasies constantly! Sometimes I yell "No!" and try to distract myself. . . .*

Sometimes I'm successful; sometimes I'm not.

FEBRUARY 20: Woke up this morning dragging myself around. . . . I almost didn't recognize Scared Mary playing with my mind. . . . She was very subtle this morning. I finally recognized her pathetic whimpering. . . . I sat her gently but firmly down, and in a loving way I let her know that I don't have to be as needy as she. I don't have to be desperate! The thought occurred to me that maybe I'm fooling myself into believing this, but who cares? It feels better!

FEBRUARY 22: Scared Mary is learning about the real world—my world. I'm trying to help her realize she doesn't have to run off to never-never land to be happy. She has to see the opportunities that already exist. Tom needs a little work, but he's a good husband, and I'm sure I have a love for him. I need to stay around and work it out, make it happen. Hear that, Mary?

FEBRUARY 23: I think if Scared Mary doesn't see me running around being scared all the time, she may learn a thing or two. I made my first attempt to be courageous. I went over and sat next to Tom and held his hand. For one precious moment Scared Mary stopped being scared!

Mary progressed with her Directed Imagination and eventually began to see Ron in perspective. He was, in fact, nothing less than a Prince Charming for her. He was going to awaken her to the bliss of love and security that was missing in her life. But as you can see from the above account, not all was so romantic. The panicky fear of the Insecure Child caused Mary to behave like a half-starved animal-child desperately clinging to Ron for fulfillment. Nothing romantic about this image!

Fortunately for her marriage, Mary realized that it was not Ron who possessed the magic — he just represented it. Once Mary began to recognize her ability to confront Scared Mary and reason with her from an adult perspective, things began to change dramatically. Whenever she began to experience her longing, she would summon Scared Mary forward and straighten her out. She began to insist on finding out how she could pursue legitimate love, not romantic projections.

The irony was that she had never even talked to Ron and knew absolutely nothing about him! He had been completely immortalized by the Insecure Child.

Mary eventually came to understand that she had a fear of intimacy that had gotten her into a passionless marriage. She was able to function in an appropriate but nevertheless lifeless way. Her obsessions over Ron reflected an attempt to compensate for her emptiness. One thing about a projected relationship — it is safe! Mary realized this by carefully observing Scared Mary. Things were much easier to visualize once she separated her healthy adult ego from these Child longings.

The type of contaminated thinking so typical of the Insecure Child can be illustrated by the school-phobic child. This is invariably a child whose parents have caved in to the child's inclination to avoid whatever becomes threatening in life. Witnessing their child's trauma, these parents just cannot imagine forcing their little one to endure such pain and anguish. They have felt their hearts break as their child begged and pleaded for relief. Ultimately these parents felt that they had no choice but to allow the child to stay home — at least one more day. This type of child embodies the essence of the Insecure Child and also the parental attitude that fosters, allows, and at times, encourages the avoidance.

This same parent-child experience is involved in habitual behavior. The ego becomes like the overwhelmed parent who just cannot tolerate the child's pain. Once this happens, the inner Child is permitted to go on and on with the habit. In Mary's "romance," she made the same mistake that the parent of the school-phobic child makes: She believed her Insecure Child. Whatever the Child told her, she accepted as factual reality. Remember that Mr. Perfect, walk-on-water Ron, was a person Mary had never even talked to! Yet Mary's Child *knew* he was the answer to her life's emptiness. The Insecure Child, as it would be with any child left to his or her own resources, will usually opt to avoid new or threatening situations, regardless of the necessity or importance such situations may hold for the child's ultimate development. The more insecure the child, the more the need to avoid.

Mary's Insecure Child wanted to avoid legitimate intimacy where it was most appropriate: in her marriage. Scared Mary found the safety of the infatuation much more alluring than the flesh-and-blood relationship Mary had with her husband. If the Insecure Child can produce anxiety and confusion, then it has a foot in the door. Once this happens, the Child begins to learn about your weaknesses, your limitations as a "parent" and as a person. The Insecure Child will always exploit your inadequacies (remember our friend the fieldmouse?). Once this is learned, then it is only a matter of time before the Child begins avoiding life.

Although the Insecure Child's pain originated in real wounds, this pain has evolved into a manipulative vehicle. It is an unconscious device now used to avoid some threatening aspect of life. Becoming an accomplice to this avoidance only perpetuates the problem. What is called for when you face your inner Child is a mature, well-thought-out conviction that life must be lived — not avoided. From this premise you can begin to become less involved in the Child's symptoms, seeing them for the first time as emotional manipulations, not current realities. There is no battling, no abusing, only strength.

The school-phobic child is told: "I understand how upset you feel, but there is no other choice. You must attend school." From your strength and conviction, the Insecure Child begins to learn about being strong. You begin to model the behavior that will ultimately encourage the Child's maturation. Remember, your eventual liberation depends on getting the Insecure Child to trust your judgment.

In Mary's desperation over Ron, her liberating response was: "I don't have to be desperate!" The key is not to fall prey to the Insecure Child's "desperate" view of what is essential or necessary, and, instead, to utilize the dispassionate, rational part of your healthy ego to decide where the truth lies. Mary had to separate herself from her Insecure

Child's conviction that Ron was the savior of her bland life. She had to protect herself from the Insecure Child's illusions. Once she understood this, she became capable of insisting on appropriate behavior regardless of the Child's hesitations.

The Spoiled Child

A second variation in Directed Imagination is called the "Spoiled Child." It is a whining, manipulative, bratty kid who has come to dominate your psyche just as an actual spoiled child rules his parents. This is the child who thinks she can make the world do exactly what she wants.

Children act this way when they have found the secret to manipulating their parents in such a way that they do manage to get whatever they want. This ability to manipulate was somehow incorporated into your development. This childhood strategy designed to handle your early world has now evolved and become entangled in the difficulties of your adult habit.

One basic difference between the Insecure Child and the Spoiled Child is that the Insecure Child manipulates by passively waiting to be rescued, while the Spoiled Child manipulates more actively by using power struggles to coerce. A child becomes spoiled when the parents have, on some crucial level, lost control. This loss of control is usually a result of parental weakness, fear, or inability to face up to and control the child. The parents just do not have the inner strength to take charge.

If a child has learned that your breaking point is the fifteenth "Why not?" then you can count on every argument going at least this distance. After all, is that not a rather cheap price for getting what the child wants? She or he already knows that victory is ultimately the result of persistence — manipulative persistence!

You can readily see how addictive behavior fits neatly into this concept. The "parent" in you (i.e., the healthy, rational ego) has lost control, while your addiction takes on the mannerisms of the Spoiled Child and wraps you around its little finger. Just thinking about habit re-formation causes this Child to resort to tantrums, arguing, and whining about how "It's too hard, and you can't make me!" Once you yield to this manipulation, you become embroiled in a power struggle that you cannot win.

The Spoiled Child is most adept at throwing tantrums. The best way to deal with them is to refuse to battle the Child. Have you ever seen a parent battling with a child?

> *Parent: "If you don't put that down, I'm going to punish you."*
> *Child: "I don't care."*
> *Parent: "You just wait till we get home!"*
> *Child: "So what? I don't care."*

. . . and on, and on, and on. You cannot win these battles because the child actually has the upper hand. The child does not care about anything you say! You as the parent will lose. The same applies to the internal Child. You can only win by refusing to battle.

When you are up against a screaming, panicked, anxiety-producing Child, your best strategy is to ignore the tantrum. Walk away and let the Child have its way. What happens to an actual child when a parent does this? The tantrum quickly fizzles. A tantrum is like a play: It makes no sense if there is no audience. Walk away from your anxiety. Be willing to persevere, and you will succeed in riding it out.

No matter how spoiled your attitude becomes, it is absolutely essential that you remember that there is a healthy adult aspect to the ego, as well as this Spoiled Child aspect. The healthy adult aspect is that part of you that is capable of handling life's responsibilities in a mature and disciplined way. You need to enlist this healthy adult aspect of the ego in order to be successful with the Spoiled Child.

When the Child whines and bellyaches about how miserable it is to break a particular habit, or how impossible it seems, the adult needs to insist on putting a stop to this whining: "You may not have another piece of cake. From now on you cannot go on running my life. I'm taking charge, and it's high time you begin to recognize it!" It is at this point that the discussion ends. The Spoiled Child can be counted on to challenge you with: "Why? Tell me why. It's unfair!" I will tell you the same thing I tell parents who are being bullied by their kids: Whenever a child is really confused and wants to know what is going on, feel free to enter into a discussion. However, if the child really is not interested in your reasons and only wants an opportunity to manipulate you, then you need to hold up your hands and say: "I'm sorry if you can't understand my demands, but nevertheless, this discussion is over."

A few examples of the Spoiled Child will give you a more complete feel for this concept.

■ FRED

Fred is an obsessive, 29-year-old man, married, with no children. His life is typified by fear and caution. He is an only child who has never made an adequate separation from his mother. He suffered from an eating compulsion that was beginning to cause him great anxiety because he felt powerless to control himself and because he was becoming morbidly fearful of having a stroke. The following was excerpted from his journal and our discussions:

> *I remembered what we had said about the Spoiled Child within me. It really was true. Every time I experienced discomfort I would, or maybe I should say the Child in me would, begin to bellyache. I can't really express exactly what he was saying, but he was always complaining about how miserable life is or how stupid this program is — just constant complaints.*
>
> *I started to talk to this Child-part of my brain. . . . At first I would try to reason with him. You know, just saying things like "I want you to calm down and not get so crazy. . . ." I soon found out that this had little effect on my frenzy. I decided to try a sort of tough-love approach. Whenever the war would begin, I would become firm. I would imagine that I was looking directly into his eyes, saying something like: "Now you just wait a minute! Who do you think you are, causing so much confusion? I want you to just sit there and listen to me for a minute. I'm going to decide to control my desires."*
>
> *I actually felt better, like my adult strength was taking over. It made me feel stronger and more in control than ever before. The Child still pulls his tantrums almost every day, but he doesn't get away with murder anymore.*

■ SAM

Sam is an automobile salesperson in his mid-forties. Married for twenty years, he has two children. His gambling compulsion has begun to jeopardize not only his job but the security of his family as well (he recently used a large home-equity loan to cover a gambling debt). His wife has been contemplating divorce, and Sam has become increasingly depressed. The constant prodding of his family finally convinced him to seek help. Recounting his story, Sam recalls:

> *After about two weeks without calling my bookie, I began to feel sorry for myself. I got a real case of the "why me's": "Why can't I enjoy myself? Everyone else has their pleasures, don't they?" The sadness changed frequently to anger and sometimes to rage. Anger at everyone! Sometimes I found it hard to concentrate or to work. I'd much rather just call in sick and stay home. Well, perhaps go to the track would be more accurate. I kept trying to remember what we had talked about, you know, about the Spoiled Child. I couldn't go very far, but I did come up with a neat name. I call him "Harry." Remember "Harry-the-Horse" from the play* Guys and Dolls?
>
> *Well, anyway, I started out by giving him a name and waiting to see what would develop. I must confess I was rather skeptical. I just couldn't imagine me talking to myself.*
>
> *Well, the opportunity came that very afternoon. I had an impulse to pick up the phone and place a bet on one of the college games, when Bam! — there he was! I put the phone down and decided to test things out. I told myself that I didn't need to make this bet.*
>
> *Harry went crazy: "Why are you doing this? It's not fair! I have to make that call! This will be the last bet. . . .*
>
> *I wrote down everything Harry said and, you know, it really was rather comical. It was just like my own kids when we get into a battle. I can't explain it, but it really wasn't me talking, you know, not even my own voice. It was this whining voice of . . . of a spoiled child. I felt embarrassed. Here I was — no, that's not true — Harry was . . . about to steal money from the family — again! You know, I've been carrying a lot of guilt around for a long time. This at least has helped me feel less like a creep.*
>
> *Harry's very sneaky. His motto is: "I won't get*

> caught." He reminds me so much of a little kid sneaking into his parents' bedroom, trying to steal coins from his father's pants hanging in the closet. That's how I felt! What an awakening! Well, let me tell you, I decided to become the man I am, not the boy. I didn't call in that bet, and I just let Harry go on with his temper tantrum: "It's just not fair! Not fair!" To tell you the truth, I almost had to laugh at what I was hearing. To think that I was being controlled by this kind of silliness!

The Spoiled Child will take every opportunity to argue with you. Sometimes the arguments can be rather convincing. Sometimes they just wear you down. Every battle requires at least two combatants. If you refuse to participate, you cannot be manipulated. When you stop squandering your precious energy in these cyclic power struggles, you will find untold strength and conviction at your command.

The Beast

Before proceeding with a discussion of the Beast, which represents the voice of physical cravings, let me first describe what I mean by the term "substance addiction." A substance addiction is evident whenever you are required at regular intervals to maintain a particular level or threshold of that substance in your body. Should this level drop, then you experience a craving.

If you and your habit fall into this category — whether your habit involves nicotine, cocaine, marijuana, alcohol, caffeine, chocolate, or sugar — accepting the truth and seeing yourself as "addicted" is an important step toward ultimate liberation.

Unbeknownst to you, a self-indulgent Beast has been living in your cellar all these years. When you are involved in a substance addiction, you give birth to a Beast. As your habit grows, so too does the Beast, until one day he, she, or it finally reaches full maturity and potency and begins controlling your life by demanding a fix. On this day you cross over the line that divides free choice from addicted compulsion.

What do I mean by a "Beast"? Think for a moment of a loathsome and altogether repulsive creature. If you cannot come up with one, let me suggest an image. If you happened to see *Star Wars: The Return of the Jedi* a few years ago, you may remember that archetypal slob, Jabba-the-Hutt. If you did not see the movie, imagine a giant sluglike creature, nothing but sleaze and nastiness, heavy lethargic eyes too swollen to hold open, the picture of narcissistic self-indulgence. Got the picture?

Now imagine a Jabba-like critter within you. Just suspend your critical objectivity for the moment; let go and *act as if* it, she, or he resides within you. If at this point your ego encounters some resistance to the technique and you find yourself becoming somewhat resistant, just remember that the key is to *act as if* there is a monster. You are not supposed to believe it! If you do believe there is a monster living somewhere inside, you may have more problems than addiction! What you have to do with any of the characters involved in Directed Imagination is to become an actor and act your script, allowing yourself to become caught up in the illusion you create.

Periodically throughout the day your monster stirs, opening an ugly eye, gripping your spirit, and demanding that you feed its insatiable need for your particular substance. You, of course, slavishly comply, often quite agreeably. If you are a cigarette smoker, for example, you may be deceived by such thoughts as "I would really like a cigarette now" or "Let me relax and enjoy a good smoke." But this is a sorry excuse for the truth. What you are really doing is keeping the nicotine Beast from getting vicious, from hurting you or making you feel uncomfortable. You feed it and it goes back to sleep — for a while! In any addiction, your life has been handed over to a monster who has taken up permanent residence somewhere within your psyche.

The irony is that for years you have probably savored the illusion that your habit has added so much pleasure to your otherwise hectic life. Rationalization, a psychological defense mechanism, can be defined as a good reason rather than the real reason. I have heard all the good reasons, but the bottom line is that your body has been invaded, your psyche has been contorted by the addictive Beast, and the reasons that come out of your mouth are distortions designed to defend the monster that, in reality, is killing you! The Beast is a parasite feeding off you, and you are sacrificing yourself for its perpetuation.

This introduction to the Beast is meant to launch you into your own imagination. Directed Imagination helps you to depersonalize your addiction, to take a step back and to view things with some objectivity. Once you are able to accomplish this, you are less likely to become a willing slave to the Beast. The insatiable addictive desire of the monster within you is not *you*. This is really the crucial point. You must separate yourself from that in you which has become so destructive. Only then will you come to understand the confused and contradictory feelings with which you have been living.

You, your ego, should never become identified with this intrusive, alien, manipulator that has become a squatter in your life. You must begin, right now, to mentally assert yourself against this destructive Beast. It makes all the difference in the world whether you say, "I can't wait another second. I have to have it [i.e., your particular substance] right now!" versus "The Beast is demanding its fix right now, and I still feel unable to resist."

Neither statement prevents you from running for your fix, but in the former statement you are identifying yourself with your habit and therefore with negativity, while in the latter statement you are able to maintain a relative perception of health and balance by stepping apart and dissociating yourself from the addiction. Whenever you achieve such a state of balance, you become much better at warding off feelings of being helpless and overwhelmed. Conversely, whenever you become disoriented and defeated by the Beast's aggressiveness, then all you feel is addictive compulsion: "I need.... I have to have.... I can't wait!"

■ DON

The following report from Don is a good example of the practical application of this imagery. Don is a middle-aged man, married, with two children, well-educated, and currently working in a very stressful job. He had been smoking for twenty-two years, averaging about two packs a day. He had tried quitting twice before, once going cold turkey and once working with a smoking clinic. Both times he reported feeling overwhelmed and smoking within the first forty-eight hours. His biggest fear was that maybe he did not have the strength and willpower necessary for success.

After discussing this program with him, I asked Don to come up with an image that would help us concretize his struggle. Although he first warned me that he was not very good at this sort of thing, he wrote the following account three weeks after he quit smoking:

> *I began to visualize my addiction as Gollum, that subterranean lizardlike thing from Tolkien's* Hobbit. *I don't remember him exactly, but my impression was that he was a sort of slippery fellow, ravaged by his desire for his ring of power. I just substituted nicotine for Gollum's ring. He was a slippery thinker also who always tried to trick people by rearranging the truth. At first I felt Gollum was an invention of my mind, more to satisfy your need than mine. But it really didn't take long before I was having long discussions, which invariably turned into arguments, with old Gollum. He was unreasonable, unyielding, and altogether a brute. Whenever I would try to interest him in my reasons for quitting, he would try to turn the tables on me, insisting this wasn't a great time to quit, or that I had to have just one more.*
>
> *Then, all of a sudden, I began to understand why you were making me do this. A light flashed on, and I understood that Gollum truly was speaking from another mind, different from mine. From this point on I began to feel separate, you know, more detached from smoking, exactly like you said! I began to see that cigarettes were Gollum's choice, not really mine. I can't explain it completely, but I really felt less confused. What he wanted and what I wanted were two different things.*
>
> *As the days continue, I feel different mentally. It's like I don't feel I can be seduced by Gollum's games anymore.*

Don was able to carry his Directed Imagination into and through his cessation experience. His quitting was without incident and, to date (more than one year later), he has been smoke-free — or should I say Gollum-free?

Recognizing Your Critters

Aside from the utility of using Directed Imagination for gaining control over destructive patterns in your life, another incidental yet significant component of Directed Imagination should be mentioned.

Recent research shows that hospitalized patients who are rewarded by the attention of nurses or doctors for moaning and whining actually report more discomfort and pain than patients who are only responded to whenever they stop complaining and show more self-control. Whenever you get seduced into becoming overwhelmed or threatened, you get frozen and give up responsibility for life's demands. When you begin to stand up to whatever is doing the complaining or bellyaching within you, you begin to cultivate an attitude that not only will put you in touch with your healthy, mature ego but will also alter your experiences as well. To put it another way, the healthier you become, the less discomfort and negativity you will experience.

You are going to need some time to reflect and take a mental inventory of your inner landscape. You need to become proficient at deciding which characterization of your addiction you are dealing with: the Spoiled Child, the Insecure Child, or the Beast. In order to glimpse the best possible view of these critters, look specifically toward the feelings and thoughts that erupt whenever you have a particularly strong craving, compulsion, or obsession. What voices and images tend to speak the loudest?

Once you have delineated your addictive character or characters, then allow the imagery to begin to bubble up. Try to visualize each character clearly. Close your eyes and develop a physical impression, a photograph of your antagonist. Be alert to these mental images because, like a shell awash at the wave's edge, you need to swoop up the image before it gets carried back to the depths. Allow your mind to become a bit more creative, less confined by your typical conventional way of thinking.

At first, simply allow these mental characterizations to float up into your mind. With some experience you will find that the images occur automatically. When you are beginning to acquaint yourself with one of these characters, try not to force it. Just adopt a receptive mental posture that allows you to grab hold of what flows by.

The experience of Directed Imagination is probably not anything you are familiar with from everyday living. Learning this technique is going to require some practice and patience before you can progress. When you first encounter these images, resist any temptation to judge them or to moralize about whether they are good enough. Go with whatever comes your way — be it a Scared Mary, a Harry, or a Gollum. Work to avoid conscious arrogance; demand respect for whatever, or whomever, you discover. Your ego is not aware of the power that exists in these productions, so try hard to avoid a know-it-all attitude and instead demand respect for the potential healing that resides in the characters of your Directed Imagination.

There is only one rule to keep in mind if you choose to give your critters names. If you are considering using the name of an actual flesh-and-blood person, someone whom you know, put this idea aside and try again. Personal or literal associations could interfere with the unique and private feelings involved in your own habit re-formation. If your Uncle Bill is the most loathsome, repugnant person you have ever met, he is still Uncle Bill with characteristics of his own that may not reflect the nature of your Beast. The more primitive and primordial the image, the better.

Denial

Perhaps you are thinking, "But why should I go to all the trouble of learning this technique? I could stop any time I want to. I don't really have a problem." This response typifies a defense mechanism called "denial." Denial allows you to pursue your addictive delights without any psychological discomfort. It allows you to postpone a confrontation with your problem by creating a smokescreen, which for all intents and purposes erases whatever addictive problem you want to avoid (incidentally, denial is more often employed by the Spoiled Child and the Beast; the Insecure Child never feels this arrogant about anything).

Whenever you have become lost to an addiction or a habit, you can only begin to find help when you have hit the proverbial "bottom." But contrary to popular notions, hitting bottom does not have to be dramatic or life-threatening. It can just as readily refer to your point of awakening. For some this may be an epiphany, a moment of insight or awareness, while for others it may come as a reaction to feeling unhealthy or out of control. In fact, it could come from reading these words! You hit bottom whenever you become humble enough to let go of denial and accept the truth about your habit.

If you are still clinging to any deception or denial regarding your particular habit, then any approach for habit re-formation is proportionately limited, if not crippled. If, on the other hand, you are willing to look at yourself more objectively, then you will be able honestly to admit the reality of your addictive problems. At this point Directed Imagination will become a most efficient technique for healing your habit.

Steps For Success

1 Begin to think in terms of Directed Imagination. Always begin an inquiry into your addictive behavior with the question: "Who in me is doing my thinking at this moment?" You will learn to refine your technique as you go along, but the experience you gain at this point will be very valuable.

2 After you have gained some familiarity with Directed Imagination, you are ready to engage in some internal dialogue. In Chapter 4 you will learn to formally document these exchanges in your journal. For now, just begin to develop a sense of working directly with your characters. Act as if these were flesh-and-blood realities. Try engaging them in conversation. Review the examples given in this chapter in order to gain a feel for these confrontations.

Resist any temptation to evaluate these exchanges. This will only lead to a kind of performance anxiety, which will limit the natural spontaneity that is necessary.

3 Learn to differentiate your characters of addiction. Keep this general outline in mind as you begin:

A. *The Insecure Child*: Tends to be passive, often looking to avoid some aspect of life or to be rescued. Typified by fear and distrust. Often associated with such states as panic, hysteria, fearfulness, depression, and impotence. When identified with the Insecure Child, your tendency is to feel overwhelmed. Once overwhelmed, you cave in to your habit. Life is just too difficult for the Insecure Child to deal with.

Famous last words of the Insecure Child: "It's too hard!"

B. *The Spoiled Child*: Typically represented by manipulation. A whiner and a complainer who tends to wear you down with tantrums. Wants to get you into a power struggle. A true tormentor who is adept at intimidation and coercion. Unlike the Insecure Child's passive approach, the Spoiled Child's approach is very active. It prefers battle and conflict to further its aims. When identified with the Spoiled Child, your tendency is to become selfish and irresponsible about your habit. The Spoiled Child manipulates your thinking into justifying your habit. You wind up saying, "Why not?

What the heck!"

Famous last words of the Spoiled Child: "It's not fair!"

C. *The Beast*: The voice of physical craving. The essence of the Beast is the ability to bully. It controls you by a kind of physical and psychological terrorism. The Beast will resort to any strategy, any manipulation, to weaken your resolve to quit. Denial and rationalization are favorite defenses of the Beast. During withdrawal, the Beast works overtime to tyrannize you through cravings, distortions, and confusion.

Unlike either the Insecure Child or the Spoiled Child, you do not usually identify with the Beast; you sense its alien presence as an intrusion into your life. The only way to avoid the Beast is to continue with your destructive habit. To pursue habit re-formation requires standing up to the Beast. The Beast is usually supported and aided by the Spoiled Child and/or the Insecure Child.

4 Begin to record your dialogues with the characters of your habit. You may want to purchase your journal at this time (see Chapter 4). Write down the date and time of each entry so that you can see patterns as they begin to emerge. Further instructions for using your journal will be given in Chapter 4, but for now, simply record your conversations as you begin to sort out your critters.

5 A good way to distinguish your characters one from another is to keep a detailed list of all their traits. In your journal make one column for the Insecure Child, one for the Spoiled Child, and one for the Beast. Under each heading, list the traits that begin to emerge from your Directed Imagination. For example:

Insecure Child	**Spoiled Child**	**Beast**
lives in fear	a real complainer	a big bully
cannot cope	tries to confuse me	panics me
thinks this is too hard	torments me	frightens me
depresses me	manipulates me	threatens me
etc.	etc.	etc.

3

DEALING WITH THE STRESS OF HABIT RE-FORMATION:
BODY NURTURING

Structuring Your Personal Program

☐ **Smoking**

Read Chapter 3 in its entirety. All three sections ("Rest," "Exercise," and "Diet") are important for smoke cessation, especially the section on "Diet." In this section become very familiar with the concept of "preventive snacking" and learn about both the High and Low Glycemic foods. This is a good time to stock up on these foods. Also pay particular attention to the effects of protein and fats.

Nicotine does act to suppress the appetite, so cravings for food are a normal reaction to the stress of nicotine withdrawal. Eating is perhaps the only substitute that can stand nose-to-nose with the craving for nicotine. Unfortunately, eating works only while you are eating. Stop eating and you are back in the chaos of nicotine withdrawal. This is precisely why so many people gain weight during smoke cessation. In a fruitless attempt to avoid the pangs of withdrawal, they become nibbling machines. While you cannot erase nicotine's cravings, you can, however, effectively counter them through Directed Imagination and preventive snacking.

Using Directed Imagination, try to figure out which character is doing your thinking when visions of sugar plums dance in your head. Whenever you are involved in a "binge mentality," you can bet you are being manipulated from within. Most likely you will find the Spoiled Child or the Insecure Child. Insist on eating only sensible foods during your moments of Child "neediness."

For most smokers, the act of cigarette smoking is deeply intertwined with most, if not all, of life's activities. During cessation, the three most dangerous situations are after meals, drinking coffee, and imbibing in alcohol. To break the tyranny of the after-dinner desire to smoke, you may find it helpful immediately after dinner to brush your teeth, tongue, and gums, followed by a mouth rinse. The Beast hates a clean mouth. If possible, minimize or substitute something else for coffee or alcohol. Herbal tea, either hot or iced, makes a great alternative.

Drinking water is a must (see the section on "Water"). It will help control your food intake, give you a glass to hold onto, help transport the nicotine from your body, and allow you to imagine that you are drowning the Beast. You may want to visualize each sip of water as a pounding surf, slowly eroding the Beast away. You may also want to take an adequate multivitamin with an added supplement of vitamin C, which has been shown to be beneficial not only when the body is under stress but also in counterbalancing the effects of nicotine.

Nicotine creates a chemical dependence that must be fed regularly. When you stop, your body will still crave these "maintenance" cigarettes. If you are like most smokers, you probably look to your habit to reduce stress when you feel a bit tense or anxious and to reward yourself throughout the day for jobs well-done (washing the dishes, adding oil to your car, finishing a report, folding the laundry). In the absence of these routine smokes, you will experience a vacuum in your life's activities. The elimination of these cigarettes will invariably elicit tantrums from your Children. Be prepared. In each of these situations, Directed Imagination can afford relief.

The *Steps for Success* are very important. I would, however, suggest that you begin your exercise program after, rather than before, your cessation date.

☐ Compulsive Eating

Read Chapter 3 in its entirety. Special emphasis should be given to the section on exercise and to the introduction to the section on diet. Although you may not be involved in "preventive snacking," the concepts contained in the "Diet" section (i.e., the physiological effects of carbohydrate foods, fat, and protein) may offer you assistance with your food plan.

Experimental evidence suggests that a significant aspect of compulsive eating is related more to environmental cues than to hunger. Simply stated, if your home is stockpiled with foods that have caused you trouble in the past, you will be more tempted to eat than if these cues were absent. Similarly, if you have gotten into the habit of eating something every time you sit down to watch television, you will need to break this connection. Make a list of all your environmental connections. See how you can anticipate these pitfalls.

The basic point of the section on "Diet" is to try to reconnect with your hunger. You need to understand food as body nourishment, not as an emotional life preserver. The more you are able to respond to your internal cues for hunger rather than to emotional or environmental cues, the better.

This is a good time to go through your pantry. Eliminate all foods that are contrary to your mature, adult intentions for sensible eating (give them away; do not eat them!). From now on, emotional

first-aid will come from your attitude, not your cupboard.
Pay attention to the *Steps for Success*.

☐ Phobias
Read all of Chapter 3, paying equal attention to the sections on "Rest," "Exercise," and "Diet." Although phobias will not chronically deplete your physical resources, it is still important to fortify yourself before attempting a confrontation with your phobic fears. Give special attention to the *Steps for Success*.

☐ Obsessive Thinking
Read all of Chapter 3. Preventive measures are important for you because of the ongoing anxiety that obsessions create. In the section on "Diet," pay particular attention to the Low Glycemic foods. These are the foods that will offer you a sense of balance and stability over a prolonged period of time. Pay close attention to the *Steps for Success*.

☐ General Compulsions/Compulsive Gambling
Read Chapter 3 in its entirety. Pay equal attention to all three sections on "Rest," "Exercise," and "Diet." Special attention should be given to the section on High Glycemic foods that may be helpful during an acute compulsive episode. Give special attention to the *Steps for Success*.

☐ Drug Addiction
Read Chapter 3, paying close attention to the section on "Diet." Make sure to stock up on both High and Low Glycemic foods. You may also want to take an adequate multivitamin with an added supplement of vitamin C, which has been shown to be beneficial when the body is subject to stress. Give special attention to the *Steps for Success*.

☐ Alcohol Addiction
Read Chapter 3 in its entirety. Pay close attention to the section on "Diet." Make sure to stock up on both High and Low Glycemic foods. You may find it helpful to take a good multivitamin with an added supplement of vitamin C, which has proven beneficial when the body is under stress. Give special attention to the *Steps for Success*.

Think back to the last time you woke up with a sore throat, fever, and runny nose. Remember your mood as you tried to drag yourself out of bed? How eager were you to start your day? Contrast this experience with the recollection (or fantasy) of an early morning workout at the gym, a sauna, massage, and shower. When you left the gym about to begin your day, you felt acutely alive, your senses more in tune with nature's beauty. What do you imagine your mood would be here? When we are feeling great, our perception of the world is totally different from the world we experience when we are a bit under the weather.

Of the two scenarios described above, which do you imagine would maximize your chances of survival during withdrawal from your addiction or habit, and which would minimize it? There is no contest. When you are feeling healthy, rested, and energized, you handle adversity differently than when you are depleted. When dealing with the rigors of habit re-formation, it is essential to employ a complete array of body nurturing techniques that will leave you feeling strong, healthy, energetic, and well-fortified. Only then can you expect your mood to be an ally rather than an enemy.

As you approach your cessation date (that point in time when you plan to quit your habit), you must realize that this moment is comprised of many previous moments of preparation and fortification. Body nurturing refers to a total experience of physical and psychological pampering and preparing. Rest, exercise, and diet are three indispensable components if you plan to reduce your risk of failure. It is easier to stand against adversity when you are feeling good. Likewise, it is easier to muster your defenses, regardless of the foe, when you feel strong, healthy, and rested.

Rest

Simply stated, your body requires sleep to function normally. Although scientists are not exactly sure how the body restores itself, intuition and experience certainly suggest that adequate sleep is essential for carrying on normal, effective living.

From a psychological point of view, dreams appear to compensate for, or balance out, the day's conflicts, anxieties, and difficulties. We know from experiments that people who are deprived of dream sleep become more aggressive, more irritable, and less able to tolerate stress. They also have difficulty with impulse control. Prolonged sleep deprivation can eventually result in such psychotic experiences as delusions, paranoia, and hallucinations. Obviously, if you are about to wage a significant battle against the characters of your addictive behavior, you cannot afford to be anything less than one hundred percent, especially in the area of impulse control!

Start by accepting the fact that sleep and rest are vital to your eventual success. With this in mind, begin to fortify yourself now, before entering withdrawal. If you have no difficulty getting to bed and falling asleep within a reasonable period of time (about half an hour), then consider allowing yourself the opportunity to sleep a bit more, especially the week leading up to your planned cessation. Do not force yourself to stay in bed. Just try either going to bed a little earlier or, if you are so fortunate, not setting your alarm clock. Remember, sleep is a vital building block for success, not an indulgence.

If you normally have trouble getting to sleep, try focusing on your pre-sleep ritual — all the things you usually do each night before retiring (e.g., feeding the fish, having a bowl of cereal, checking the thermostat, locking the doors, brushing your teeth, and so on). This routine may begin as much as an hour or two before you actually go to bed. The pre-sleep ritual is important because it helps you wind down before going to sleep. In evaluating your pre-sleep ritual, consider turning off the television a little earlier and heating a glass of milk (milk contains tryptophan, which acts as a natural relaxer). Stay away from late-night caffeine products such as coffee, tea, hot chocolate, or colas. Begin to set up a regular bedtime and stick with it.

Once you do go to bed, do not fall prey to worry or ruminations. Here is a golden opportunity to practice your Directed Imagination. Simply declare: "I'm sure you guys want to go right on worrying, but it's time to turn the lights off now." Realize that as your body and psyche prepare for sleep, you become less effective at handling problems and worries. Just make a pact with yourself to let go until morning. Allow yourself to trust that you will not neglect your responsibilities, especially not now that you are getting used to using your Directed Imagination.

Naps and other restful experiences also come under this category. Not everyone can incorporate a nap into their busy schedule, and not everyone benefits from napping. If an afternoon siesta has worked to refresh you in the past, try hard to arrange for some nap time. Rest in general — be it soaking in a warm tub or lying back and listening to music — has this same restorative effect on the body and mind.

Your body experiences two kinds of metabolism: anabolic and catabolic. "Anabolic" refers to constructive or energizing activities, and "catabolic" refers to destructive, enervating activities. It is basic biology: Things either build you up or tear you down. Begin to differentiate your experiences into these two categories. For example, your anabolic list (things that build up your resources) might include listening to the relaxation portion of the tape you will prepare in Chapter 5, practicing meditation, doing yoga, taking a bubble bath, praying, listening to Mozart, knitting a sweater, arranging some flowers, or watching the clouds drift by. Catabolic activities (those that deplete your reserves) might include paying bills, worrying, being late, going to the dentist, arguing, or taking on too many responsibilities. Especially now, when you are preparing to move into your withdrawal experience with fully charged batteries, make sure you choose an anabolic way of life.

Exercise

Aside from rest, the body also needs exercise. For many people who have established a sedentary lifestyle, getting moving again is very hard. Robert Maynard Hutchins, the great president of the University of Chicago, once quipped, "Every time I get the urge to exercise, I lie down for a while until the urge passes." The body (your body!) does, however, yearn to be exercised. If you are over forty and overweight, however, you may want to check first with your physician before engaging in any strenuous physical activity.

We were not designed to participate in life from the sidelines. This is, unfortunately, what we have become — a society of spectators, content to turn on our television sets and allow professional athletes to do our running, jumping, and throwing while we cheer them on. As our psyche participates vicariously, our body sinks further into the couch. When "our" team wins, we are elated, and when they lose, we become depressed. I actually knew a man who would call in sick for work on Monday morning if "his" team lost Sunday's game.

Turn off the television and join the world of movement. Give your body a taste of the real thing. It does not matter whether you choose jogging, walking, swimming, biking, or skiing. Just get going.

When your body begins to regain its intended shape and use, when your heart and lungs begin to respond to the increased oxygen and improved circulation, you will find that a sense of well-being will replace your typical sense of blah. Your sleep will improve, along with your alertness, stamina, and general vitality. A word of caution, though: Avoid strenuous exercise just before going to sleep. Remember your pre-sleep ritual and your need to wind down.

One last point about exercise: Some people fear that they will become hungrier because of the increased physical demands on their bodies. You will not become hungrier when you exercise. In fact, as your body adapts to your exercise regime, you will actually burn calories more effectively and efficiently, which helps you with weight loss.

You can start by walking. Just get out there and take a ten-minute walk. Some report that as little as twenty minutes of aerobic exercise three times a week is all you need for cardiovascular fitness. Ultimately, if you hope to control your weight, you should strive to build up to twenty or thirty minutes of exercise daily.

One rule of thumb: Never strain. Listen to your heart and muscles carefully. Do not worry if you need to slow down or rest from time to time. If you experience muscle aches or soreness, quit for the day. The beauty of exercise is that it is a process. You do not have to achieve any particular goal on any particular day. There is always tomorrow.

As a two-time New York city marathoner, I can tell you that when I began to run some years ago it was all I could do to reach the end of my block. If you had told me I would someday run more than twenty-six miles, I would have chuckled in disbelief. The workouts did, however, gradually increase over the years. My time spent running is a precious thing to me now. It sets the tone and pace for my day. I never know how far or how fast I will go, but the result is always the same — a feeling of calm and serenity. Finishing a run and coming home to a family waking up, with all the chores of getting lunches made and homework papers stuffed into knapsacks, never puts so much as a dent in this glow.

I pass this on to you from personal experience and conviction. Stay with some form of exercise, and year by year you will only get better, stronger, and healthier.

Diet

This section is applicable to all habit re-formation. Even if your problem is a food addiction or an eating disorder, these nutritional concepts may be incorporated into your eating plan. Before discussing the general nutritional aspects of the program, let me first say a few words about compulsive eating.

Compulsive Overeating

Directed Imagination does not offer a specific weight loss diet, but it works very well as an adjunct to such programs as Overeaters Anonymous or Weight Watchers. My particular emphasis for compulsive eating is to establish, through Directed Imagination, more "hunger consciousness." As simple as it may sound, it is essential to re-connect eating with hunger.

The compulsive aspect of eating is really a symptom, a strategy for coping. Through confrontations with your characters, you will need to find out what role food is playing in your psychological life. Along with this information, you need to be able to differentiate real hunger from the Child's or the Beast's hunger. The biggest problem you face is that your unconscious leads you to the misperception that you are biologically hungry (versus psychologically hungry) and that eating will make you feel better. True, eating does make you feel better. Unfortunately, these feelings are short-lived, available *only* while you are eating. Once you stop eating, the negative feelings creep back. Sometimes guilt is added to make things worse. The biggest misperception is that you can escape your bad feelings through food.

Sticking to your scheduled meals will require not being duped by false hunger or by promises of psychological salvation. However tempting it may be to take a time out from life's difficulties through food, you must realize that it is one of your compulsive characters who is trying to plant those suggestions. Suggestion, as you will see in Chapter 5, is a powerful tool. You can easily become convinced you are starving if you listen to the erroneous suggestions of the Beast or a Child.

If you define your eating as "compulsive" — if you binge or starve yourself, if your eating is totally out of control — your task will be to understand the demands of your characters and then to assert your adult consciousness into the equation. This is particularly true if your eating has become somewhat impulsive and reflexive. You will learn to see food objectively rather than subjectively. Once you begin to understand the inner, psychological demands of your characters, you can begin to alter the emotional connections you have made with food.

Dealing with Withdrawal Depletion

As you are probably well aware by this point, habit re-formation is an arduous experience that will tax your mind and body in many ways, quickly depleting the chemical reserves needed to deal with stress. You should anticipate and be ready to compensate for this depletion, not only through Directed Imagination, exercise, and rest, but also nutritionally.

Certain carbohydrate foods are metabolized by the body in such a way that they are actually tranquilizing to the system. Such natural drugs can go a long way in dulling the edge of anxiety and the stress related to habit re-formation. Ample evidence exists that in a stressed state the brain quickly uses up its supply of serotonin, an inhibitory neurotransmitter that reduces neuron activity and thereby promotes relaxation, tranquillity, and sleep. High-carbohydrate meals increase the amino acid tryptophan that, once in the brain, is converted into serotonin. The operative word for our purposes is *carbohydrate*.

Carbohydrates come in two varieties: starches, called "complex carbohydrates," and sugars, or "simple carbohydrates." Starches and sugars can be either natural (found in foods as they come from the earth) or "refined." Refined foods are any foods that have natural carbohydrates added to them. The sugars are small molecules that are digested and used quickly by the body, while the starches, which can be composed of thousands of branched molecules, are much more slowly absorbed by the body. Starches are found in varying amounts in such foods as whole grains, legumes, fruits, vegetables, rice, and potatoes. Natural sugar, although contained in such sources as fruits, vegetables, and milk, is more often associated with such sweeteners as honey, molasses, fructose, and raw sugar. When you extract sugar from its natural sources and add it in concentrated amounts to such nutritionally bankrupt items as cakes, cookies, and candies, then it is referred to as "refined" or "processed" sugar.

When it comes to reducing stress through diet, a simple sugar has one single important advantage over a starch: its rate of absorption. Sugars are absorbed more rapidly in the gastrointestinal tract than are starches, thereby quickly offering relief from an acute, stressful experience associated with a specific craving.

But before you begin to stock up on Gummy Bears and Twinkies, let me caution you about foods that cause blood sugar to rise too rapidly. When blood sugar is sent skyrocketing by certain sugars, a severe insulin response causes blood sugar to fall just as rapidly. When this occurs, you are left feeling tired, depleted, and still hungry. If you happen to be prone to hypoglycemia, then your reaction could be even more severe.

There is, however, one circumstance that warrants this quick sugar pick-up in spite of the let-down reaction that follows: Whenever you are caught off guard by a craving attack and need to reestablish a sense of balance. During the period when you are going through substance withdrawal, these attacks, although short-lived, can be quite nasty, evoking panic, confusion, and physical discomfort. When gripped by a craving, you are totally justified in following a whatever-it-takes philosophy to get you through. You may reach for a can of soda or a candy bar. (If you are fighting an eating habit, however, then unfortunately this philosophy would be contrary to your aims and should not be employed. I will shortly introduce you to a form of preventive snacking that can easily be incorporated into any dietary regime.)

But keep one thing in mind as you wolf down your snack: Although a craving usually has you convinced that it will never end, the truth is that most physical cravings (especially for nicotine) will peak within one to three minutes and then begin to recede. The first day or so of withdrawal may seem like Dante's *Inferno* only because these cravings are strung close together, giving you the impression that relief will never come. This is the Beast at its best (or should I say worst?), bombarding you with a volley of cravings designed to quickly discourage the faint-hearted.

Do not get snared by this rather typical trap. Instead, with stopwatch in hand, enter the boxing ring with the Beast. Each round is represented by a three-minute craving, and only when the round is over will you be able to seek the asylum of your corner. As an unknown underdog prizefighter, Rocky Balboa's only goal (in the movie *Rocky*) was to go the distance with the champion of the world. You, like Rocky, can come out the winner if you just stay in the fight, refuse to give up, and go the distance. Keep in mind that the Beast does not have a knock-out punch. It can defeat you only if you quit.

If you are dealing with a thought disorder rather than a substance addiction, you will find it useful to adopt a similar strategy. Although not a craving per se, some of the anxiety that accompanies obsessive ruminations takes on the same characteristics as a physical craving. Here is an excerpt from a journal of a man obsessed with irrational fears of having a heart attack:

> *I felt tense when I woke up this morning. After breakfast I began to feel anxious. My hands began to shake, my legs felt weak. . . . I could only think about my heart. . . . My body can't take this stress any longer. . . . I began to perspire. . . . My breathing became difficult.*

The basic difference between a physical craving and a psychological craving is that the physical craving is determined by the blood level threshold of the addictive substance, while the anxiety associated with obsessive thoughts occurs more randomly. Another major difference between the two is that anxiety reactions often exceed the three-minute limit typical of nicotine and other substance withdrawals. In fact, it is not uncommon for anxiety attacks to last for hours.

If you are observant, however, you will notice an ebb and flow in the intensity of anxiety within each period. It is critical to minimize the anxiety long enough to employ your Directed Imagination. What you want to avoid at all costs is doing anything that increases the anxiety. Here is where preventive snacking is needed.

The Glycemic Index

With both thought and substance cravings, the whatever-it-takes approach to nutritional aid applies. But there are alternatives that offer you some distinct advantages. One such alternative is to snack on what are called "high-glycemic carbohydrates." They offer rapid sugar absorption, resulting in the tryptophan-serotonin conversion described earlier. One additional bonus these particular carbohydrate foods offer is that you can choose foods that are calorically minimal and nutritionally beneficial.

Even if you do not give a hoot about nutrition, gaining weight is probably an altogether different matter. Just mention weight gain to someone trying to quit smoking, for example, and it usually sends their anxiety level right off the Richter Scale. So the dilemma remains: how to spike the serotonin production of the brain without ingesting hundreds of calories.

The answer comes from a rating scale called the *Glycemic Index (G.I.)* (see page 66), which is used to identify how fast certain foods cause sugar to rise in the blood, as well as how long the level stays elevated. Using the *Glycemic Index*, we can readily see that certain foods, such as carrots, have a high rating, almost three times as high as ice cream. Your intuition may be that the ice cream will get you through the tight spots more easily than carrots, but the reality is that those carrot sticks will do a better job of it with a tremendous saving in calories. Using the chart, you can arrange your snacks to coincide with your concern for weight.

For those of you who, because of the fear of gaining weight, still feel apprehensive about carbohydrates, let me point out that contrary to popular notions, if you first eliminate refined sugar products from your diet (e.g., cakes, doughnuts, candy bars, sugared sodas, etc.), carbohydrates can actually help you lose weight! The only reason such foods as breads and potatoes have become such naughty words among the diet conscious is because of what often gets put on them — sugars such as jam or jelly, and fats such as butter, sour cream, or cheese spreads. Carbohydrates are no more fattening than protein and happen to be considerably less fattening than fat. Experimental evidence suggests that carbohydrates are preferentially used as a source of energy by the body rather than being stored as fat reserves. Carbohydrates provide substantial nutrients with enough bulk and fiber to keep you satisfied psychologically as well as physically.

Glycemic ■ Index (g.i.)*

FOOD	G.I. VALUE	FOOD	G.I. VALUE
Breads:		Banana	79
Pumpernickel	70	Cherries	32
Rye	89	Grapefruit	36
Wheat	99	Grapes	62
White	100	Orange	66
Whole meal	89	Orange juice	67
		Pear	40
Breakfast Cereals:		Plum	34
All-Bran	71–76	Raisins	93
Cornflakes	119		
Muesli	96	**Legumes:**	
Oat bran — uncooked	84	Baked beans	60
Oatmeal — cooked	85	Butter beans	39–52
Porridge oats	71–96	Chick peas	46–52
Puffed rice	132	Green peas, dried	32–68
Shredded wheat	97	frozen	55–74
Weetabix	109	Haricot (white) beans	44–84
		Kidney beans	27–65
Cereal Products:		Lima beans	115
Barley	31	Peanuts	10–19
Buckwheat	74	Red lentils	25–43
Bulgur	65	Soy beans, dried	20
Millet	103	canned	22
Cookies:		**Miscellaneous:**	
Oatmeal	78	Baked goods	75
Plain crackers (water biscuits)	91	Tomato soup	55
Dairy Products:		**Pasta:**	
Ice cream	52	Macaroni, white	
Milk, skim	46	(boiled 4 min.)	64
whole	49	Spaghetti, brown	
Yogurt	52	(boiled 15 min.)	61
		white (boiled 15 min.)	46–72
Fruit:		white (boiled 5 min.)	45
Apple	53	protein-enriched	38

* Adapted from David J. A. Jenkins and Alexandra L. Jenkins, "The Glycemic Index Fiber, and the Dietary Treatment of Hypertriglyceridemia and Diabetes," *Journal of the American College of Nutrition*, vol. 6, no. 1 (1987): 11–17. Copyright © 1987, by John Wiley & Sons, Inc. Reprinted by permission of John Wiley & Sons, Inc.

   Also adapted from Anita B. Lasswell, "Nutrition and Diabetes Mellitus," *Nutrition Clinics*, vol. 3, no. 5 (1988): 13–14. Used by permission of J. B. Lippincott Co.

FOOD	G.I. VALUE	FOOD	G.I. VALUE
Snack Foods:		Carrots	133
Corn chips	99	Corn	87
Potato chips	74–79	Parsnips	141
		Potatoes, new red, boiled	81
Sugars:		baked	135
Fructose	29–35	instant	116
Honey	126	Rice, brown	81
Maltose	152	instant (boiled 1 min.)	65
Sucrose	85–92	instant (boiled 6 min.)	121
		white	83
Vegetables:		Turnips	104
Beets	93	Yams	74

Up to this point we have been discussing only the foods rated high on the G.I. scale, foods that offer acute relief from the stressful cravings associated with withdrawal. For the longer, more drawn-out periods of anxiety associated with obsessions, or the weeks following cessation from a substance addiction, a high level of fortification and stamina are required. Not only must you be vigilantly prepared for an occasional craving to crop up, but you must also be ready for the transitional requirements involved in breaking any incidental habits that may have become associated with your addiction.

In this regard, an even greater role is played by the foods lower on the G.I. scale. These are the typical complex carbohydrates that keep blood sugar stable for much longer periods of time. This is your preventive snacking, which, in order to be effective, must take place at regular intervals throughout your withdrawal experience. As you can see from the chart, your choices do not have to be highly caloric. Apples, oranges, oatmeal, spaghetti, breads — all make great stress-prevention foods. A good snack is a sweet potato or a yam cooked in the microwave for about ten minutes, then wrapped in foil and nibbled on throughout the day.

One word of caution before you begin to plan your carbohydrate menu. Whenever you intend to carbo-snack for any of the benefits mentioned, *do not* add protein to your snack. Protein contains certain amino acids that will compete for absorption with tryptophan, preventing it from reaching the brain. A slice of whole wheat bread or a bagel may sound terribly lonely without a hunk of liverwurst sandwiched in the middle, but if you add the meat, you add a negative to a positive (to say nothing of all the extra calories). One cancels out the effects of the other. Your carbohydrate snacking must stay pure if you are going to gain the aforementioned benefits.

A final word on diet in general: Become more conscious of the fat content in what you eat. Regardless of whether it is a protein or a carbohydrate, food high in fat is digested slowly compared to other foods and tends to end up as fat deposits rather than as expended energy. The longer digestion time requires a significant amount of blood to be siphoned from the brain and redirected toward the stomach and intestines to assist in digestion. It is this added demand for blood that causes you to feel sluggish, drowsy, and moody. As you have no doubt begun to surmise, you are not going to need any additional contributions toward feeling out of sorts during your habit re-formation experience. Avoid adding problems by learning to read the labels on all packaged foods in order to minimize or at least cut back on the fat content in your diet.

Water

Along with your meals and preventive snacking, it is also essential to drink water as often as possible. Water will help control your food intake, as well as unwanted calories. Drinking at least six to eight glasses of water a day will keep your body well hydrated. Not only will a well-hydrated body help burn off fat, but it will also assist your kidneys in flushing out the various accumulated toxins in your body. This flushing is most crucial for substance addictions, but it is also helpful in weight reduction (especially in low-carbohydrate diets that contaminate the blood with ketones). For variation you might try some of the new fruit-juice-flavored seltzers, adding a twist. They are really great tasting and have no calories.

The importance of maintaining regular, nutritious meals during your habit re-formation experience cannot be overstated. Preventive snacking reflects one aspect of a total dietary balance that is achieved through conscious awareness and effort. This concept of balance goes beyond diet and includes your physical and mental status as well. Whenever imbalances are created, the body tries to compensate, usually calling in assistance from other valuable resources. The medical term for the process whereby the body is able to maintain its own physiological equilibrium is "homeostasis." Just as the body knows to send white blood corpuscles to assist the healing of a cut, so too the body's homeostatic proclivity reacts to any imbalance, physical or psychological.

Whenever the Beast takes over your body during the throes of physical withdrawal, or when the anxiety of obsessive rumination has depleted your system, your homeostatic mechanisms easily become overwhelmed. When your body becomes depleted by anxiety and tension, you enter a state of physical and psychological disequilibrium. Using Directed Imagination and the various techniques suggested in this book, you will eventually get to a point where, instead of discharging your system, you will begin charging it.

Preventive nutrition provides you with an interim means of accomplishing this charging. In essence, preventive snacking allows you to directly affect the imbalance and provide the chemicals (serotonin) necessary for normal functioning. Preventive nutrition will not change your underlying problem, but it will provide enough restoration to allow you to pursue your task of habit re-formation more enthusiastically.

Steps For Success

1 *Rest.* Begin to become rest-conscious. If possible, try to increase your hours of sleep, especially the week preceding your planned cessation. Make a list of all your anabolic (restorative) activities (e.g., meditation, yoga, relaxation tape, hot bath, listening to music, and so on). Contrast this list to a catabolic (depletion) list (e.g., arguing, paying bills, cleaning the cat box, etc.). Be creative and add to your anabolic list things you may want to try. Keep these lists as reminders for when your cessation begins.

2 *Exercise.* This is a good time to begin an exercise program. If you are overweight and/or over forty, this is also the time to check in with your physician. Remember to start easy, perhaps walking about ten minutes a day. Gradually increase your workouts to about twenty minutes, three times a week. Particularly effective are such exercises as walking, jogging, biking, swimming, and skiing. If you have the option, try to exercise outside in the fresh air rather than in a stuffy gym or on a basement treadmill. Although you may initially consider exercise a catabolic activity, it will not take long before you realize how rejuvenating it actually is.

3 *Diet.* Begin by familiarizing yourself with the *Glycemic Index*. The foods listed with high G.I. values offer acute relief from stressful cravings and similar withdrawal experiences. The foods with low G.I. values are of special value for the longer, more drawn-out periods of anxiety associated with thought habits such as obsessions or for the long-term stamina required in the weeks following cessation from a substance addiction. Remember, if your snacking is primarily for prevention of stress, do not add protein. Become conscious of the fat content of your diet. Increase your water intake to flush out toxic substances.

Decide which foods are most appealing to you and begin to stock up prior to your planned cessation date. Clear out those foods that are not on your plan for sensible eating.

4

VIEWING YOUR HABIT FROM ANOTHER PERSPECTIVE:
JOURNAL

Structuring Your Personal Program

☐ **Smoking**
Read Chapter 4 in its entirety.

You have already begun to keep a record of your dialogues with the Beast, the Spoiled Child, and/or the Insecure Child (as instructed in Chapter 2 *Steps for Success*, Step 4). You should also pay close attention to any strong cravings for cigarettes (e.g., times of day, circumstances, etc.) for future reference. Understanding your characters of addiction, especially your Beast tendencies, before cessation will prove invaluable. Your journal should attempt to document your pattern of cravings along with the patterns of sabotage that occur throughout each day. The *Steps for Success* outline what material should be included in your journal entries.

As you approach your cessation date, prepare a structured-format journal for use during the first four days of withdrawal. The section on "Setting Up Your Journal" gives an example to follow. You can taper down to twice-daily recording for days five through eleven, and then to once daily for days twelve through eighteen. Thereafter you can continue to write in your journal as you find it helpful.

☐ **Compulsive Eating**
Read all of Chapter 4, paying close attention to the differences between structured and unstructured formats.

You have already begun to keep a record of your dialogues with the Insecure Child, the Spoiled Child, and the Beast (as instructed in Chapter 2 *Steps for Success*, Step 4). You should also pay close attention to any strong cravings (e.g., particular foods, times of day, circumstances, etc.) for future reference. Understanding your characters of addiction, especially your Beast tendencies, before cessation will prove invaluable. Your journal should attempt to document your pattern of cravings along with the patterns of sabotage that occur throughout each day. The *Steps for Success* outline what material should be included in your journal entries.

As your cessation date approaches, prepare a structured format for the first four days of cessation (see "Setting Up Your Journal" for an example to follow). You will need to leave extra space at mealtimes to record *everything* you eat, in order to be honest with yourself. Withdrawal's Beastly cravings can create quite a chaotic fog. This is not the time to trust your perceptions.

Once you have gained some confidence in your capacity to deal with your characters and cravings, you can modify the amount of structure to suit your particular needs. I would suggest a tapering-off structure: Days five through fourteen would consist of three recordings per day with an optional listing of foods and hourly checks; from day fifteen on, you would write once a day without a food list (though you should record any inappropriate foods). This gradual tapering will provide the best system for building strength and confidence in your Directed Imagination.

☐ Phobias

Read Chapter 4. You have already begun to keep a record of your dialogues with the Insecure Child and/or the Spoiled Child (as instructed in Chapter 2 *Steps for Success*, Step 4). You should also pay close attention to any strong patterns of fear (e.g., times of day, circumstances, etc.). The *Steps for Success* outline what material should be included in your journal entries.

Although you may elect to use an unstructured journal (see the section on "Setting Up Your Journal"), if your phobias are strong and you expect chaos throughout your day, I would suggest that you make at least three entries per day.

☐ Obsessive Thinking

Read Chapter 4. You have already begun to keep a record of your dialogues with the Insecure Child and/or the Spoiled Child (as instructed in Chapter 2 *Steps for Success*, Step 4). You should also pay close attention to any strong patterns of obsession (e.g., times of day, circumstances, events that appear to trigger your thinking, etc.). The *Steps for Success* outline what material should be included in your journal entries.

Although you may elect to use an unstructured journal (see the section on "Setting Up Your Journal"), if your obsessive thinking is strong and you expect chaos throughout your day, I would suggest that you make at least three recordings per day.

☐ General Compulsions/Compulsive Gambling

Read Chapter 4 in its entirety.

You have already begun to keep a record of your dialogues with the Spoiled Child, the Insecure Child, and perhaps the Beast (as instructed in Chapter 2 *Steps for Success*, Step 4). You should also pay close attention to any strong patterns of compulsion (e.g., times of day, circumstances, triggering events, etc.) for future reference. Understanding your characters of addiction before cessation will prove invaluable. Your journal should attempt to document your pattern of obsession along with the patterns of sabotage that occur throughout each day. The *Steps for Success* outline what material should be included in your journal entries.

As your cessation date approaches, if your compulsion is particularly strong and you expect substantial chaos, you may elect to use a structured format for your journal with hourly check-off boxes (see "Setting Up Your Journal" for an example to follow). If your compulsion is less intense, an unstructured format with three recordings per day may be sufficient.

☐ **Drug Addiction**
Read Chapter 4 in its entirety.

You have already begun to keep a record of your dialogues with the Beast, the Spoiled Child, and/or the Insecure Child (as instructed in Chapter 2 *Steps for Success*, Step 4). You should also pay close attention to any strong cravings for drugs (e.g., times of day, circumstances, etc.) for future reference. Understanding your characters of addiction, especially your Beast tendencies, before cessation will prove invaluable. Your journal should attempt to document your pattern of cravings along with the patterns of sabotage that occur throughout each day. The *Steps for Success* outline what material should be included in your journal entries.

As you approach your cessation date, prepare a structured-format journal for use during the first four days of withdrawal. The section on "Setting Up Your Journal" gives an example to follow. You can taper down to twice-daily recording for days five through eleven, and then to once daily for days twelve through eighteen. Thereafter you can continue to write in your journal as you find it helpful.

☐ **Alcohol Addiction**
Read Chapter 4 in its entirety.

You have already begun to keep a record of your dialogues with the Beast, the Spoiled Child and/or the Insecure Child (as instructed in Chapter 2 *Steps for Success*, Step 4). You should also pay close attention to any strong cravings for alcohol (e.g., times of day, circumstances, etc.) for future reference. Understanding your characters of addiction, especially your Beast tendencies, before cessation will prove invaluable. Your journal should attempt to document your pattern of cravings along with the patterns of sabotage that occur throughout each day. The *Steps for Success* outline what material should be included in your journal entries.

As you approach your cessation date, prepare a structured-format journal for use during the first four days of withdrawal. The section on "Setting Up Your Journal" gives an example to follow. You can taper down to twice-daily recording for days five through eleven, and then to once daily for days twelve through eighteen. Thereafter you can continue to write in your journal as you find it helpful.

Take a moment to reflect on the flow of your thoughts. You will discover that your concentration tends to cluster around specific themes or patterns of thoughts. These thought-trains are coupled together in such a way that, like an actual railroad train, you can track the caboose all the way back to its engine simply by recognizing each preceding car in the chain. Consciousness reflects this same linear or sequential thinking. The reason you can find your way back to the "engine" in your thoughts is because conscious thinking follows a basically rational mode of operation (i.e., one thought connects to a preceding thought that connects to its preceding thought, and so on).

Consciousness is an effective problem solver. The human race's evolutionary success has depended on the development of a mode of conscious thinking that not only keeps us involved in the sights, sounds, and smells of our physical world but also provides us with a means of surviving the more abstract challenges of a hostile world. You can imagine what an advantage it has been for a species actually to be able to anticipate future events or learn from past experiences.

Although superior to any computer yet designed, conscious thinking is never without some interference or competition of thoughts. You are always paying selective attention to your world, trying to focus on one aspect of your perceptual field rather than another.

Say, for example, that I were to ask you to ponder the ultimate meaning of life. You might begin by sifting through various intellectual or rational possibilities. All of a sudden a low-flying jet makes a pass over your house, causing you to glance up. A vague feeling of annoyance about being interrupted and startled begins to percolate. You may simultaneously begin to notice that your stomach has just begun to tighten and your pulse has quickened. As the seconds tick away and the tide of stimuli recedes, you find yourself reminded of your original focus: figuring out the meaning of life. You come back to this line of thought and proceed once again. In a short while frustration begins to creep in. You begin feeling more and more overwhelmed as you dig deeper, trying to penetrate this difficult question. At first you barely notice it, then it becomes more apparent: a dull, throbbing headache. The headache distracts you as you once again shift gears from intellectual thoughts to more practical thoughts such as "Should I get an aspirin?"

What the above illustrates is that, at any given moment, your intended focus is always competing for conscious attention. You are a sensory machine continually processing information, not only from your mind, but also from your internal and external worlds as well. Like a butterfly flitting from flower to flower, you leap from thought to thought, or as in the example, from thought-to-distraction-back-to-thought. Eventually, if you persist, you do figure things out and get things done.

When you dive into withdrawal's turmoil, your desire for concentrated focus becomes only one fish swimming in a school of many competing thoughts, reactions, and distractions. Among these competitors you are sure to find Beast thoughts, Spoiled Child thoughts, and Insecure Child thoughts. Unfortunately, the competition does not stop there. Along with these thoughts, you are also blessed with an array of physical reactions that are the by-products of habit re-formation. Discomfort, irritability, nervousness, headaches, and the like all begin to elbow their way into your already crowded perceptual field.

Directed Imagination allows you to avoid getting swamped by this deluge of stimuli. When you learn to focus on one specific characterization of your withdrawal experience, you will hear only one voice rather than a cacophony of distractions. Imagine that you are on a conference call with five or six other people. Each person is talking simultaneously. Try as you might, you just cannot make sense of who is talking or what is being said. There is just too much competition. One by one, each person hangs up until you are left with one last person, one last voice and no distractions. This is the voice you can finally communicate with. Using Directed Imagination, you will seek only the voice of the Insecure Child, the Spoiled Child, or the Beast. With this focused communication you will finally be in a position to confront each character and negotiate your eventual liberation.

Surviving Withdrawal's Three D's

Although withdrawal's three D's — distractions, distortions, and discomforts — can never be totally eliminated, you need not be discouraged. Directed Imagination, as well as the techniques introduced in this and the next chapter, will teach you to effectively neutralize these mental distractions. You do not have to eliminate the other voices; you just have to get them to speak more softly so you can focus on whichever character is center stage at the moment.

Once the distractions quiet down, you can concentrate on the voice that concerns you — the voice of your addictive character. (Remember, do not just look for one character. These critters can take turns working you over.) If you become derailed by your thoughts or reactions, you will gently, without panic or hysterics, take yourself by the arm and guide yourself back to your designated path of habit re-formation, back to your Directed Imagination dialogue. Allow yourself to trust the process. If you start off with patience, I assure you the path will become more familiar and more accessible day by day.

To ensure your ability to maintain conscious focus during the rigorous demands of habit re-formation, I am going to suggest two techniques for eliminating unwanted mental distractions. Both techniques are what I call psychological "filters." They are capable of allowing designated thoughts and feelings through while trapping unwanted or intrusive thoughts. Once trapped, these destructive thoughts are systematically neutralized.

This chapter deals with the first filter: keeping a journal. Chapter 5 will introduce the second filter: hypnosis. These filters are the final components of your structural preparation.

The Journal Advantage

To understand the therapeutic usefulness of keeping a journal, we must first contrast the process of thinking with that of writing. Writing is a curious phenomenon that at times appears to be a bit less conscious than thinking. Have you ever had the experience where your pen just seemed to take off, as if something within you had finally found a conduit for expression? Often this "something" can be quite creative and insightful. Writing appears to be more a product of the right hemisphere of the brain than the left. The right hemisphere is more involved with a kind of intuitive, holistic synthesis. The left hemisphere is more responsible for logical and analytical ways of thinking. Writing is not illogical, but it is capable of becoming more intuitive and spontaneous than your usual mental reflections.

Clues

Whatever the physiological underpinnings, writing offers the capability of revealing the intricacies of your habit. Fundamental clues into the nature and pattern of your addiction will at times seem to pop off the page. Views not always apparent to your limited conscious view will be consistently brought forward through the process of writing.

Frequently when you keep a journal, there will be a genuine sense of discovery. Sometimes your journal will reveal startling, even revolutionary, ideas. At other times you may experience the "Ah-ha!" feeling of spontaneously seeing the light. Not that every word is an epiphany, but when looked at thematically and as a whole, a piece of writing usually offers insights exceeding the sum of its parts. The experience is not unlike standing too close to an impressionistic painting. All you can make out are shimmering, swimming dabs of color moving from one hue to another without rhyme or reason. If you back up a few paces, the random patterns of brush strokes and color immediately congeal into such familiar vistas as ponds, flowers, or trees. Only from this vantage point are you able to interpret the artist's intention.

Only by witnessing the more complete view of your habit revealed in your journal do you increase your ability to anticipate what lurks on your path. At the very least, your efforts at keeping a journal will give you a sense of the connection between your life and your struggles. Without this connection you walk around moaning about how this habit has invaded your unsuspecting life. You become the passive victim, ruled by your habit. When, instead, you understand the habit as a misguided aspect of your thinking and feeling — a Beast, a Spoiled Child, or an Insecure Child, all of which you must take responsibility for — then, and only then, can you begin to actively take charge of your life.

Dialogue

The journal and Directed Imagination are both techniques that require some practice and confidence before you can obtain maximum results. For this reason you should begin to employ both prior to your planned cessation date. Once acquainted with the internal characterizations of your habit through Directed Imagination, you can begin methodically to shift the balance of power from your inner critters to your healthy ego. This shift of power allows you to make choices that will, ultimately, liberate you from compulsion. Your journal, aside from offering an invaluable tool for self-monitoring, serves primarily to amplify the process of Directed Imagination.

Your first concern when making a journal entry is to record any dialogue between you and one of your characters. If you followed Step 4 of the *Steps for Success* in Chapter 2, you have already been doing this. Any and all exchanges are grist for the mill and should be written down in a descriptive narrative. Start off by recording any verbal exchanges you have between one of your characters and your ego. Be as clear and specific as possible. Include all of your feelings as well:

> *The Beast grabbed me. I felt helpless and frightened as it held me down and insisted on being fed.*

Or:

> *The Spoiled Child's arms were flailing, her face was beet red, her legs were kicking. She really seemed desperate. All the time she was yelling: "It's not fair! It's not fair!" I felt overwhelmed and angry.*

If, as so often happens, you cannot recall exactly what was said, allow your intuition to fill in the blanks. For example, say you were trying to recall a conversation you had had with the Insecure Child. You remember that the Child was whining about not being able to make it or about it being too hard to go on. You just cannot remember the gist of your reactions. You might reflect for a moment on how you might have responded, or you can simply ask yourself what you would say now if you were speaking to this Child: *Sure you can! Just keep listening to me. I'll help you.* Filling in the blanks is a way of enhancing your Directed Imagination work that in no way reduces the effectiveness of the technique.

Experimentation

Once you have written down the narrative between you and your characters as accurately as possible, begin to branch out and speculate about any aspect of your experience. You might, for example, write about who your character reminds you of or about similar experiences you may have had. This is a time for spontaneous or even impulsive writing.

When you see an opportunity to paint a mental picture with your words, take it. Accept and trust that your reactions, your words, and your language are all valid means of describing the total experience between you and your characters. Let go of doubt and find what works best for you. This is the imaginative part of Directed Imagination. You may choose to experiment with some creative forms of expression — perhaps a drawing depicting the Beast's menacing appearance or an abstract water color reflecting the emotional turmoil you experience. Poetry, music, sculpting, and the like can all be vehicles to amplify your words and your experience. These are your subjective perceptions. Perceptions are not right or wrong — they are interpretations, personal views. There is no need to be cautious here.

You will find that your writing becomes an indispensable guide for recalling and highlighting past confrontations with your internal characters. Whatever you do, do not try to be profound — just write down your reactions. In fact, the simpler and more straightforward the expression, the easier it will be to digest. You are not trying to impress anyone, just to heal yourself!

When you approach your journal writing in this manner, you will end up with a more complete document, one that captures the flavor and intensity of the exchanges between you and your Beast, Spoiled Child, or Insecure Child. When rereading and trying to digest your report, you will be able to re-experience these exchanges in a very vivid, direct way.

Filter

Aside from exposing your Beast and Child tendencies, your journal also acts to filter out extraneous and troublesome stimuli (e.g., "Did I remember to tell Harry about the invitation?" or "What time was that dental appointment?"). This filtering allows you to stay focused on the primary issue of habit re-formation. Whenever you make an entry in your journal, first check to see exactly who — or in the case of the Beast, what — may be controlling your thinking. Record all pertinent information relating to your Directed Imagination efforts. This done, go on to take a reading of all your reactions, both physical and emotional.

You will find that the simple act of writing down your feelings may begin to release you from them. This reminds me of an old joke about a patient who, after talking incessantly throughout the session, not allowing the therapist to get a word in edgewise, gets up, shakes the therapist's hand, and, while walking out the door, replies, "Thanks! You really helped me today." Sometimes, rather than answers, we just need a vehicle, or an outlet, for expressing our emotions.

Whenever an intensity of emotion is locked in your head, psychic pressure is generated. Eventually this pressure causes your psychic thermostat to register too much emotional build-up. This causes the thermostat to click on, allowing a dissipation of pressure. Eventually the pressure is lowered through the psyche's thermostatic (homeostatic) processes (e.g., defense mechanisms, distractions, dreams, etc.). When your temperature returns to normal, the thermostat clicks off. At this point you can once again resume normal conscious intentions — at least until the next conflict presents itself.

When you write out your feelings, you are not just sitting around waiting for your emotional furnace to explode. Instead of passively waiting for your body to regulate the situation, you choose to take charge and determine when to work out and let go of these destructive emotions. As you write, your emotional conflicts and distractions are transferred out of your head and body and onto the paper. This cathartic release from tension, fear, or pain is a major reason why your journal is such a valuable tool during habit re-formation.

Confession

Journal writing becomes a kind of confessional, with all the benefits Roman Catholics have known for centuries. The mere act of expressing your secret transgressions, doubts, fears, and the like allows you to begin to dissociate yourself from them. Whenever something is contained or confined within the psyche because of fear or the possibility of reprisal, it exerts pressure. Once these secrets are shared or exposed, you are no longer affected in the same way. At this point typically your pressures and anxieties subside. Freeing yourself from any and all emotional clutter is certainly a potent way of insuring that your conscious intent and your ability to make appropriate choices remain clearly focused.

Free Association

Initially, quite a few people experience some form of writer's block. They do not know what to write, or they feel that they have nothing to say.

In the course of psychotherapy if a patient reports being blocked or frozen and not able to come up with a single thought, I might point to the office door and ask him or her to tell me all about the door — whatever comes to mind regarding my door. After I reassure the patient that I am quite serious in suggesting such a ludicrous assignment, she or he will usually begin with understandable trepidation: *I see a solid wooden door . . . walnut . . . brass doorknob. . . .* If the thoughts begin to wander away from "door-thoughts" (as they always do), I encourage the person simply to follow these thoughts wherever they lead: *I wonder who else will be coming through that door when I leave? Sometimes I wish I didn't have to leave. . . . I can never feel safe.*

This, of course, is the Freudian technique of "free association." You simply allow your thoughts and associations to roam freely from topic to topic without conscious scrutiny. With free association it truly does not matter where you begin, as long as you begin.

The psyche knows what it needs to maintain balance. Unfortunately, through the distortions of habit and addiction, the healing voice of the psyche is not easy to hear. Directed Imagination provides you with a broom for sweeping away the debris of addictive thinking. Learning to free associate in your journal is a way of adding bristles to your broom, thus increasing its effectiveness. Once you begin to sweep away the clutter, your innate propensity for homeostasis can begin to guide your life. Only at this point can you move more spontaneously toward what is meaningful and healthy.

Free association, in essence, is a tool for "stumbling" into the subtle voices of your psyche. If you are like most people, you will resist this mental stumbling around. Your rational intellect prefers a much more focused problem-solving effort to such random meandering. Until you begin to realize and trust the benefits of free association, you might feel a bit awkward. This is quite natural and expected. Do not be deterred. With a little practice and persistence you will find a wealth of insight at your fingertips. Remember: If your rational approach was so effective in the first place, you would have figured out a way to be habit-free long ago. Free association offers you an alternative way of gaining important data. Because of its novelty and spontaneity, it is less susceptible to the addictive distortions that often confine and confuse your thinking.

Think of your typical rational problem-solving approach as being like the sun. As long as it is dominate in the sky, the infinite mystery of the universe is concealed from view. Only when the sun sets, do you get a glimpse of the vast enormity of what lies beyond. If you keep looking exclusively to rational thought for direction, then you will never see beyond your immediate solar system.

With a little practice, courage, and trust, you can allow your pen to race across the page, pouring out spontaneous reactions to your inner drama — all this without the crippling constraints imposed by your tunnel-visioned rationality. What do you have to lose? So what if nothing important comes forward? You are not any worse off. Then again, look what you have to gain!

Privacy Allows Honesty

One thing that will greatly inhibit your ability to free associate and go with the flow is whether or not you keep your material private. If you have any sense that someone will some day read what you write, you will be inviting worry about your literary image. Not only will you be more conscious of your grammar and spelling, you will certainly be more conscious of, if not paranoid about, the content of what you write.

A friend recently reported to me that while pursuing one of the more popular liquid diet plans, she was required to keep a diary of all she ate. When I asked her if she found this technique helpful, she replied without missing a beat, "Oh no, I lied." It turned out that she lied because of the social pressure of presenting her diary each week to her group. In fact, it was common practice within the group to fabricate the results. The plan fostered competition among the dieters, and no one wanted to admit that she was too "weak" to keep up with the rest.

Protect what you write by taking whatever precautions are necessary to ensure your privacy and make you feel secure. Some people choose to carry their journals with them in their briefcases; others hide them away in drawers. Regardless of how relaxed you may be about self-disclosure, you cannot take any chances with unconscious sabotage. So keep this a private matter, and you will not go wrong.

Your journal can help you become an opportunist, ready to capitalize on any advantage that furthers your cause of liberation. Be warned, however: Only an accurate reflection of your inner experience will be helpful. Could you imagine having a mirror that reflected only what you wanted to see and not how you actually looked? Once the novelty wore off, there would be no motive to go on looking in it. You would never get the appropriate feedback necessary for proper grooming. This is precisely what the dieting woman managed to accomplish by lying about her eating in her diary.

Just keeping a journal will offer you nothing unless it is honest and accurate. Any deception or subterfuge in your reporting voids all guarantees. Incidentally, let me remind you that not all deception is consciously perpetrated. This whole area of impression management, whether it is in your writing or in your social interactions, is fertile territory for the Insecure Child to create mischief. Even if you take precautions to ensure privacy, the Insecure Child can counter any security measure by insisting: "You never know.... What if I die and my drawers are cleaned? What if... ?" The Insecure Child feels most protected when allowed to live behind a facade. This is a world of image and illusion where God forbid that anyone should find out you are failing, are not doing well, or are less than perfect!

The quest for perfection is fundamentally a quest for control, and a neurotic need for control is the parent of distrust. The more insecure the Child, the less likely she or he is to follow a path that is difficult or unknown. This is especially true when following the inner path of habit re-formation. This path is sure to take you through the brambles of chaos, confusion, and frustration.

The Insecure Child feels there is no choice. He or she simply must control everything and everyone or feel intense anxiety. Because of the Child's fear of losing control, you can see why any danger or novelty is fear-provoking. One way to lessen the Insecure Child's interference with your journal writing is to avoid any reflecting while you write — just free associate.

If you do succumb to the Insecure Child's interruptions, use your Directed Imagination for reassurance. Help the Child to understand that all of the necessary precautions have been taken to ensure the Child's need for safety and security. The Child must come to understand that the disclosures contained in your journal are absolutely necessary. Insist on being honest. Choose to represent yourself in your journal as you are, without deception. This kind of courage is impossible when the Insecure Child controls your thinking. It is available only when your mature, healthy ego takes charge. Once you have addressed the Child's insecurity, then it is time to assert your will and carry out your legitimate right to continue.

Feedback

Think of your journal as a chronicle of thoughts extracted from the chaotic, emotional moment for viewing more dispassionately at a later time when you can digest and interpret their meaning. The journal becomes a mirror of the unconscious that reflects the patterns of manipulation typically hurled at you by the Beast and its cohorts, the Spoiled Child and the Insecure Child. Directed Imagination is a means of getting acquainted with each of your internal characters, while your journal maps their strategies of manipulation. One look at the map can reveal potential bottlenecks as well as the shortest routes. Using your journal as a map will provide you with the capacity for anticipating your habit's route of attack as well as your own road to freedom. You will never be caught off guard again.

If, for example, your journal begins to reveal an Insecure Child's pattern of hysterical thinking (i.e., self-doubt, insecurity, and panic), you can use this information to formulate a plan of resistance. You may, for instance, retrieve your pre-prepared list of reasons for making your choice (see the Chapter 1 *Steps for Success*). Then you could, every hour or so, read your list over. It could become a personal mantra, a way of insisting on rational rather than emotional thoughts, of confirming for the Insecure Child that you are in control and that everything will be okay. You could do this until the Child's panic recedes. Whatever ploy your addictive characters use, be it subtle or sadistic, if you are able to anticipate the patterns of assault, you are fifty percent home free.

Thus, your journal becomes a source of personal feedback. Conceptually, feedback is a very valuable psychological tool, capable of guiding and shaping your reactions based on the revelation of your inner experiences. Using your journal notes as feedback can help you understand your changing patterns of feelings, mood swings, irritability, and general discomfort. By carefully reviewing your notes, you will see that certain behaviors or thought patterns typically bring chaos and misery, while other thoughts or behavioral strategies consistently bring a sense of tranquillity. In essence, you are allowing your journal to provide you with the necessary feedback to mold and shape you into a success.

Through your ongoing feedback, you will learn those strategies that regularly work and those that do not. As you progress by fine tuning this information, you will eventually wind up with a reliable system of things you can do, feel, or think to promote positive feelings and to defuse destructive thoughts. No more playing peek-a-boo with your destructive, and heretofore unconscious, voices.

No one can give you a prescription ahead of time as to what will work specifically for you. You must, instead, learn to make the necessary adjustments as you proceed, based on the feedback you get from your journal. These adjustments will ultimately guide you toward the truth.

Setting Up Your Journal

Journal writing is a very personal enterprise, which will also require some intuitive judgments on your part to decide what format best suits your needs.

You will need to purchase a suitable book. Some people prefer a bound blank book; others choose a looseleaf binder. Some want lined sheets; others do not. Find a format that you will enjoy using. Perhaps you will also want to buy a special pen so that your writing will flow comfortably and easily.

Do not trivialize this task. In fact, I suggest you ritualize the entire procedure. I have become a firm believer in the psychological value of ritual. Whether it is a graduation ceremony or a funeral, rituals allow us to go beyond ourselves and into ourselves in a way that we could not hope to fathom consciously. So find a suitable book and a special pen. Keep in mind that each time you make an entry, you are going to try to ceremoniously accept the revelations of your psyche with nothing less than a reverent attitude.

Unstructured Format

If your habit re-formation will not involve intense cravings and falls into the category of obsessive thinking, compulsions such as gambling or spending, or phobias in general, your journal can be fairly unstructured, reflecting instead your own personal preferences for recording your experiences. You need to be guided by your habit, the amount of distress, and the amount of conflict you experience.

Where your habit causes substantial chaos throughout your day (e.g., chronic anxiety obsessions, repetitive compulsions like handwashing, cleaning, gambling, or spending), frequent journal entries will be helpful. Although hourly monitoring may not be necessary (unless you want to be very conservative), I would suggest making entries three times a day. Where your habit causes relatively minor disruptions to your daily life (e.g., some phobic situations that you can avoid, minor obsessions, or compulsions), once-a-day recording will probably be adequate.

But be sure to write at least once a day in your journal and to review your previous entries regularly. Your entries can be summations of the day's struggles along with Directed Imagination encounters. Going beyond habit re-formation, you will find that the techniques you are learning in this book will assist you in dealing with life's more routine and unavoidable difficulties. Keeping a journal beyond the point dictated by habit re-formation can become a valuable asset to your ongoing psychological growth.

Structured Format

A structured format usually works best during withdrawal from an addictive substance (e.g., nicotine, marijuana, caffeine, etc.), or when physical cravings are anticipated such as with weight reduction, eating disorders, or specific food addictions. Any substance — such as sugar, chocolate, chewing gum, fatty baked goods, or soda — can become part of a psychological addiction based not exclusively on physical or chemical dependency but on psychological habit as well. Depending on your perception of how intense you expect withdrawal's cravings to be during the first few days, you must decide to what extent you will structure your journal.

A structured journal provides a definite advantage during the initial stages of withdrawal when your cravings will be at their peak. An intense withdrawal experience can leave you feeling confused and disoriented, with little incentive to go on. A structured journal, by requiring regimented efforts on your part, will keep you constantly and actively involved in habit re-formation, Directed Imagination, feedback, and reinforcement. As the days progress, the structure is lessened. You reach a point where, according to your estimation of progress, you can allow your journal to become a more spontaneous and natural expression of your inner world.

Below (see page 91) is an example of an hourly format that represents the most extreme example of a structured journal. A structured format is an arbitrary layout that dictates when and how you record your journal entries. If you choose to follow a structured format during your initial period of cessation, each hour of at least the first four days of withdrawal should be represented. After four days of hourly monitoring, the structure can taper to twice-daily recording for days five through eleven, and then to once-daily recording for days twelve through eighteen. Following day eighteen no specific structure is suggested, but you are encouraged to maintain an ongoing journal of at least one entry per day to ensure continued growth and success. The structure you eventually select for your long-term journal can be a synthesis of what worked well for you during your habit re-formation experience.

To set up an hourly journal, refer to the example. Each hour of cessation appears in the left margin, beginning with your designated quitting time and going for ninety-six hours, or four days. Next to each hour is a box. These will be used for checking off each hour in which you have been free of your habit. After each box leave at least eight blank lines for your entries, more if you feel prolific or if you have large handwriting.

You are not required to make an entry every hour — in fact, you will find during your initial period of cessation that at times any task may be too burdensome — but leave lines even for the night hours. You may be awake, and writing in your journal will help you silence the voices of your critters. Basically, the hourly format is designed to encourage and promote as much involvement in your habit re-formation as possible.

Rewards

As you progress through your withdrawal, you will keep a record of every successful hour of cessation by checking off each of the hourly boxes. One reason for starting your program at night is that, come morning, you get to check off at least seven or eight boxes. That has got to feel pretty good! This process of checking off the boxes one by one provides a snapshot of your progress as well as a reward/reinforcement system. Alcoholics Anonymous has a pin for the person who achieves ninety days of sobriety, Weight Watchers has a ribbon for the first ten pounds lost, and you have your accumulation of check marks.

These rewards become highly valued and symbolic expressions of your efforts. They really do help! Hour by hour you begin to feel a

Structured ■ Journal Format

Thursday, October 1:
9 p.m. ☐ _____

10 p.m. ☐ _____

11 p.m. ☐ _____

Midnight ☐ _____

Friday, October 2:
1 a.m. ☐ _____

sense of momentum and progress that is expressed by the steady progression of check marks celebrating each successful hour. You cannot help feeling a glowing sense of pride and accomplishment as you flip through page after page of checked-off hours.

You may want to consider starting your own reward system for successful hours, days, or weeks. But do not be naive. If your problem centers on food, you do not want to treat yourself to an ice cream cone. If you are a gambler, do not plan a day at the track. Perhaps a new tennis racquet, a golf club, a book, a bouquet of flowers, or a record album. Rewards need not be expensive. They could be simply hugs from a friend or encouraging notes to yourself. Stock up on some colorful stickers or stars for your journal (or calendar) and allow your pages to reflect each success. Buy your rewards ahead of time and arrange either with someone else or with yourself to dispense them only after you have reached certain goals. Never underestimate the power of such rewards.

■ JOHN

To best illustrate the process of setting up and maintaining a journal, I have selected a structured format used for smoke cessation, primarily because of the intensity of this particular withdrawal experience. It was written by John, a single man in his late twenties. John had been a heavy smoker for about twelve years. Regardless of which format you select — structured or unstructured — the example of John's journal that follows is a useful illustration of the basic mechanics of journal writing and Directed Imagination. Only entries that were filled in are included here; the time periods left blank are omitted.

Day One

8 a.m. ☑ *Haven't had a cigarette since dinner last night. Listened to my hypnosis tape, watched television, and went to bed. Twelve hours smoke-free already!*

9 a.m. ☑ *Had a cup of coffee. Felt my first real craving. I can only call it painful! The Beast is hurting for a*

cigarette. So am I! Help!

10 a.m. ☑ *Terrible hour. All Beast! I feel like I'm being eaten alive. I feel tense all over.... Want to scream and it's only the beginning!*

12 noon ☑ *Felt panic, tried to use Directed Imagination, but wasn't too successful — couldn't concentrate. Went for a walk.... Got through panic.... Afraid to eat lunch, tried a low G.I. snack (oatmeal and skim milk).*

4 p.m. ☑ *Too difficult to write!*

5 p.m. ☑ *High G.I. snack (dry cornflakes).*

7 p.m. ☑ *Tough day! I've been fighting most of day with Beast cravings. I sense it's the Beast, but I can't get a clear image yet of what it could be.... Just a kind of gnawing feeling all over. I'll be glad for a clear thought about anything! Going outside for a walk helps. Meals kill me. Supper was the worst. Managed to get up from table, brush teeth, and walk dog. Feeling frazzled, cranky, angry!*

8 p.m. ☑ *High G.I. snack (bag of corn chips and Coke).*

9 p.m. ☑ *Directed Imagination requires big effort — too big! Tried relaxation.... Hard to focus.... Wish I could sleep.*

10 p.m. ☑ *High G.I. snack (plain crackers and orange juice).*

Day Two

9 a.m. ☑ *Woke up feeling very bad — sad. I'm so edgy .... Can I take this? Sounds like Spoiled Child stuff. Hungry.... Ate big breakfast (no coffee — substituted herbal tea with three teaspoons of honey for high G.I. snack). Took a walk right away.*

11 a.m. ☑ *High G.I. snack (tablespoon of honey). Cravings all the time.*

12 noon ☑ *Had good lunch (low fat).... Friend and I played tennis. That felt good! Still quite miserable.... Been drinking water every half hour or so.*

3 p.m. ☑ *Hi G.I. snack (three small russet potatoes, microwaved with apple cider vinegar and seasoning). Snacks seem to help.*

5 p.m. ☑ *Constant desire.... When will relief come? ... Somebody, help!*

6 p.m. ☑ *Spoiled Child was writing 5 p.m. entry! Had a few moments of sanity. Went with friend for a walk....*

It is very clear from rereading my notes that walking seems to be best thing for me at this point.

8 p.m. ☑ *After supper all bad feelings return. . . . Felt like crying. When I asked the question "Who is it in me that feels like crying?" guess who I found? A Spoiled Child! I'm going to call him the "little Imp." Hopefully will get to bed early tonight.*

Day Three

9 a.m. ☑ *Woke up feeling miserable but with a sense of accomplishment! Maybe, just maybe, I'll do this!*

10 a.m. ☑ *Light breakfast. . . . Brushed teeth. Mouthwash really helps! Took dog for walk.*

11 a.m. ☑ *High G.I. snack (one banana).*

12 noon ☑ *Lunch difficult, but I was ready for my monster craving. I actually stood up right after my last bite and headed for the bathroom and a quick mouth rinse.*

4 p.m. ☑ *BIG CRAVING! Thank God, I could get into my Directed Imagination. Beast reminded me of a pit bull. He just gnaws at me, shaking his head back and forth, trying to tear me apart. Couldn't talk to him. . . . Have to figure out how to take command.*

5 p.m. ☑ *Tried a low G.I. snack (one-half cup peanuts).*

7 p.m. ☑ *Cravings seem to be coming more randomly rather than all the time. Thank God for small favors!*

10 p.m. ☑ *Tried relaxation techniques. Got me through. . . . Feel tired and pathetic, but a bit less crazy . . . only a bit.*

Day Four

10 a.m. ☑ *Having easier time with the pit bull. . . . Call him Spike. Having a harder time, however, with the little Imp. He keeps trying to convince me that life stinks. Felt empty, called [girlfriend]. She helped me write down some great reasons for quitting: joining a gym, smelling better, looking more attractive. . . . I keep the list in my back pocket. Sometimes I just pat my back pocket to remind me of all the reasons. . . .*

11 a.m. ☑ *Breakfast was rough this morning (still!). . . . I tried to drink coffee again — within three sips I wanted to say the hell with everything and light up. No*

VIEWING YOUR HABIT FROM ANOTHER PERSPECTIVE ■ 95

more coffee today! Went for walk with dog. . . . Talked to neighbor. . . . Got over coffee's effect.

12 noon ☑ *I'm better at discrediting Spike. With the Little Imp I'm always doubting my ability. I know, I know, it's the Little Imp that uses this as a manipulation.*

2 p.m. ☑ *Guess what? A new character! I call him Con-Man. Con-Man gives me a pitch about smoking, for example, "Go ahead take a cigarette, cut it in half . . . just prove to yourself you can handle it . . . just one time." I almost listened!*

4 p.m. ☑ *Con-Man and Spoiled Child seem to work together. The good news is that I seem to be developing a stronger attitude. Yea! I can also use my Directed Imagination more effectively.*

5 p.m. ☑ *Intense craving. . . . I imagined myself picking up this huge stick. . . . Spike hated that. Made some corn flakes, milk, and honey for a high G.I. snack.*

7 p.m. ☑ *I seem to be handling meals better — fingers crossed.*

9 p.m. ☑ *Low G.I. snack (half a grapefruit). Reread 2 p.m. account of Con-Man. I'm ready. My walks really help clear my head.*

Day Six

[Note: At this point John elected to shift to once-a-day recording.]

Back to work today! Feel more optimistic. Con-Man and the Little Imp are still regulars. Haven't seen Spike around for awhile. . . . I think I'm much smarter now. My stick is always handy for Spike, should he get crazy with me. Work was okay. Everyone very supportive. I really feel like things are moving along. I've focused mainly on lower G.I. snacks throughout the day: peanuts, apples, plums, yogurt. I still flip-flop from feeling strong to feeling weak, but I don't think the Little Imp really has the same power anymore.

Day Nine

Cravings seem tamer — almost without any punch. I felt strong today! Work went okay. Listened to hypnosis tape today to confirm my resolve. I've increased my walking to one mile before work and one mile after work. My dog seems to be getting into the spirit. . . . My sleeping has really been great. I wake up feeling so much more rested than before. No more headaches for quite a few days now. My head feels so much clearer. No more morning cough. I feel healthy!

Day Twelve
Found out my job is being terminated. . . . The Little Imp jumped on my back in an instant: "What's the use? You might as well smoke. . . . Who cares? . . . You can't handle this pressure. . . ." The Little Imp came as a big surprise to me. Felt disoriented. . . . Got home and had a good scream and cry. Called [girlfriend]. . . . *Going to bed now. Thank God today is over!*

This was the end of John's eventful experiences. His journal from this point on reflected a steady progress toward liberation. Spike, the Little Imp, and Con-Man were rarely mentioned again and, for all intents and purposes, had lost their potency.

As you can see, John's process was clearly an evolution of strategies. Those things that helped (taking a walk, Directed Imagination, etc.) were repeated, while those that offered little or no relief were abandoned. John made use of his structural support quite well (e.g., hypnosis, Directed Imagination, preventive snacking, exercise, etc.). Perhaps the single most important aspect of John's journal was his persistence each day, both in reading through his accounts and continuing to make frequent entries. This tenacious attitude is the only way to derive the full essence of the feedback available from your journal.

Steps For Success

The following is only a suggested format for organizing your material. As long as you include the necessary material, the actual physical layout of your journal becomes a secondary concern.

1 Begin by identifying and writing down your Directed Imagination information:

A. Write out your dialogues with your internal characters. Just record whatever conversations take place between your characters and your ego. Use your imagination to fill in any blanks or gaps in your memory.

B. Add any pertinent comments as to what you observe (e.g., *Beast is trying to pressure me* or *My Spoiled Child is using that same manipulation again*). Any creative expression you choose can be employed to amplify your Directed Imagination.

2 Record your physical reactions (e.g., headaches, nausea, etc.).

3 Record your emotional reactions (e.g., anxiety, tension, depression).

4 Free associate. Record any insights or interpretations that emerge. Allow yourself to freely speculate. Give yourself as much freedom here as you choose.

5 As you approach your cessation date, if your guidelines in *Structuring Your Personal Program* suggest a structured format, prepare your journal pages for at least the first four days. You should have hourly boxes and writing space for 96 hours. If your habit involves food, see special instructions in the guidelines for Compulsive Eating.

6 Once you reach your cessation date, use your journal to record your encounters with your characters of addiction and to monitor the strategies that work and those that do not (e.g., preventive snacks, exercise, hypnosis tape). Be sure to check off each hour of cessation.

7 The hourly structured format should be used, as indicated in *Structuring Your Personal Program*, for the first four days of withdrawal. After that, for days five through eleven, twice-daily recordings should be sufficient. From the twelfth day on, you can probably just write once a day. If you choose to continue writing in your journal, it can become a permanent resource for psychological growth.

8 Establish at what point(s) you are entitled to some rewards. List these dates either in your journal or on a calendar. Arrange with a friend to give them to you, if you wish.

5
CHANGING YOUR FOCUS:
HYPNOSIS

Structuring Your Personal Program

☐ **Smoking**

Read Chapter 5 thoroughly. Pay particular attention to "The Circle." This technique can be used to counter every craving for nicotine. Read through "Preparing Your Tape" and the *Steps for Success* carefully before recording the "Induction Script."

Listen to the induction portion of your tape as often as possible in the time leading up to your cessation date (at least once a day for three days — more if you feel you are resisting hypnosis). This portion of the tape is designed to relax you and to prepare you for the hypnotic suggestion. When used by itself, it becomes a useful tool for general relaxation and anxiety reduction.

Before your cessation date, record the "Suggestion Script for Smoking." You will begin your cessation by listening to the entire tape.

☐ **Compulsive Eating**

Read Chapter 5 carefully, paying particular attention to "The Circle." This technique can be used to counter every craving for food. Read "Preparing Your Tape" and the *Steps for Success* carefully before recording the "Induction Script."

Listen to the induction portion of your tape as often as possible in the time leading up to your cessation date (at least once a day for three days — more if you feel you are resisting hypnosis). This portion of the tape is designed to relax you and to prepare you for the hypnotic suggestion. When used by itself, it becomes a useful tool for general relaxation and anxiety reduction.

Before your cessation date, record the "Suggestion Script for Compulsive Eating." Begin your cessation by listening to the entire tape.

☐ **Phobias**

Read Chapter 5, giving special attention to "The Circle." This technique can be used to combat your particular phobias. Read "Preparing Your Tape" and the *Steps for Success* carefully before recording the "Induction Script."

Listen to the induction portion of your tape at least once a day for three days — more if you feel you are resisting hypnosis. This portion of the tape is designed to relax you and to prepare you for the hypnotic suggestion. When used by itself, it becomes a useful tool for general relaxation and anxiety reduction.

When you feel comfortable with the hypnotic induction, record the "Suggestion Script for General Habit Control," inserting your particular phobia wherever the word "habit" is used. You may choose to consider the first time you listen to the full tape as inaugurating your complete commitment to the program.

☐ Obsessive Thinking

Read Chapter 5 thoroughly. Pay particular attention to "The Circle." This technique can be used to interrupt your obsessive thinking. Read through "Preparing Your Tape" and the *Steps for Success* carefully before recording the "Induction Script."

Listen to the induction portion of your tape at least once a day for three days — more if you feel resistant to hypnosis. This portion of the tape is designed to relax you and to prepare you for the hypnotic suggestion. When used by itself, it becomes a useful tool for general relaxation and anxiety reduction.

When you gain confidence in the use of hypnotic induction, record the "Suggestion Script for General Habit Control," inserting the phrase "obsessive thinking" wherever the word "habit" is used. If you want a specific event to mark your complete commitment to this program, let it be the first time you listen to your completed tape.

☐ General Compulsions/Compulsive Gambling

Read Chapter 5 carefully, paying particular attention to "The Circle." This technique can be used to counter your compulsive desires. Read "Preparing Your Tape" and the *Steps for Success* carefully before recording the "Induction Script."

Listen to the induction portion of your tape once a day for three days — or longer if you feel yourself resisting hypnosis. This portion of the tape is designed to relax you and to prepare you for the hypnotic suggestion. When used by itself, it becomes a useful tool for general relaxation and anxiety reduction.

Before your cessation date, record the "Suggestion Script for General Habit Control," inserting your specific compulsion wherever the word "habit" is used. Listen to the completed tape to inaugurate your commitment to conquering your compulsion.

☐ Drug Addiction

Read Chapter 5 thoroughly. Pay particular attention to "The Circle." This technique can be used to counter every craving. Read through "Preparing Your Tape" and the *Steps for Success* carefully before recording the "Induction Script."

Listen to the induction portion of your tape as often as possible in the time leading up to your cessation date (at least once a day for three days — longer if you feel you are resisting hypnosis). This portion of the tape is designed to relax you and to prepare you for the hypnotic suggestion. When used by itself, it becomes a useful tool for general relaxation and anxiety reduction.

Before your cessation date, record the "Suggestion Script for Alcohol and Drug Addiction," inserting your particular addiction where indicated. You will begin your cessation by listening to the entire tape.

☐ Alcohol Addiction

Read Chapter 5, paying particular attention to "The Circle." This technique can be used to counter every craving for alcohol. Read "Preparing Your Tape" and the *Steps for Success* carefully before recording the "Induction Script."

Listen to the induction portion of your tape as often as possible in the time leading up to your cessation date (at least once a day for three days — longer if you feel yourself resisting hypnosis). This portion of the tape is designed to relax you and to prepare you for the hypnotic suggestion. When used by itself, it becomes a useful tool for general relaxation and anxiety reduction.

Before your cessation date, record the "Suggestion Script for Alcohol and Drug Addiction," inserting the word "alcohol" where indicated. Begin your cessation by listening to the entire tape.

Hypnosis began with the German physician Anton Mesmer (1733–1815), whose theory of animal magnetism was an attempt to establish harmony in his patients by correcting what he felt was the body's unequal distribution of nervous fluids. Mesmer offered many remedies for his patients. One particularly exotic method employed a kind of tub with protruding handles that patients could hold onto in order to receive a "magnetic flow." To enhance this flow, Mesmer would play music and walk around in silk robes, adding to the overall mystique. From these not-so-humble beginnings grew hypnosis as we know it today.

Interestingly enough, Mesmer's patients were helped in spite of his rather fantastic devices and theories. They were helped because they believed in him and his animal magnetism. Herein lies the essence of the healing potential that we find in today's hypnotic technique: If you believe, if you are willing to suspend critical judgment and go along with the suggestion, you will be hypnotized. Simply stated, if you cooperate with the suggestion, you will benefit from hypnosis. If, on the other hand, you indulge a skeptical attitude and wind up muttering, "Nothing is happening. I knew it wouldn't work!" then your self-fulfilling prophecy will invariably leave you empty-handed.

Your Right Foot Is Getting Heavy

To illustrate the cooperative spirit necessary for hypnosis, take, for example, the suggestion that your right foot is getting relaxed and heavy. Cooperation means that, to the best of your ability, you suspend any critical, conscious thoughts. You agree to *act as if* your right foot were, in fact, heavy and relaxed. It is the same concept you learned to employ when dealing with the characterizations of Directed Imagination. You, in essence, decide to go along with the suggestion as an actor accepts a script and becomes the character. The more the actor becomes the character, the more convincing the performance. The same is true with hypnosis. The more you let go and accept the suggestion, as if it were actual and true, the more you will benefit.

If you happen to be a bit obsessive, it is very important for you to understand the phrase "to the best of your ability." Everyone's mind wanders, especially at first. If you demand perfect concentration on and compliance with the suggestion, then at the slightest distraction you will feel as if you have blown it. As long as you are willing to guide yourself gently back to listening and cooperating as soon as you become conscious of being distracted, you can avoid this pitfall.

Take a moment to try it out. Imagine that your right foot is becoming heavy. Just let go and allow your right foot to become heavy. Take a few seconds to increase this heaviness. Remember, everyone knows your right foot is not actually becoming heavier; you are only agreeing to feel it *as if* it were heavier. Beginning to feel it? Okay, now try to lift your right foot. Notice how very different, if not difficult, it has become to lift? Now relax your foot and allow it to feel normal again.

Practice this little exercise often. If you can become proficient at feeling your foot become heavy, you will understand exactly what is required of you during your hypnotic experience. If, on the other hand, your right foot does not grow heavy, you need to suspect resistance on your part. Your foot will not get heavy on its own — you allow the feeling of heaviness by cooperating with the suggestion.

The more you allow this experience to take place and the more you practice, the better you will get. Let us continue with the example of allowing your right foot to grow heavy. As you begin to concentrate, you may have some initial success in allowing a feeling of heaviness to radiate through your foot. Then, for no apparent reason, you may lose it. The next time you try, your foot again grows heavy, but this time it remains heavy much longer. Perhaps the third time you try, your foot remains heavy until you decide to return it to its normal condition. Hypnotic progress is a cumulative process.

Not only is your ability to follow suggestion improved by practice, but the depth of your trance is also linked to these efforts. If you have difficulty allowing your foot (or hand, or leg, or whatever) to get heavy, just keep practicing until you discover the way to let it happen.

Hypnosis is essentially a relaxation or focusing technique. Some think of it as an exotic New Age or esoteric Eastern practice. While it is similar to focusing techniques used in many religious traditions — including Christianity and Judaism —to center one's attention on God, it can be used simply to relax yourself and to focus your energies on overcoming an addiction, a habit, or a compulsion.

Demystifying Hypnosis

No one really knows why or how hypnosis works. Theoretically no concise explanation has evolved. All hypnotic techniques share one common denominator: the ability to narrow one's consciousness. Whenever you achieve this narrowing of consciousness, you become hyperfocused, capable of harnessing and channeling a great deal of psychic energy into one pursuit, such as healing your habit.

How, for example, can one explain a mother's sudden ability to lift a car off her trapped child? The only plausible explanation lies within the mind's capacity for absolute focus of energy and desire that, under the right circumstances, can be harnessed for a single purpose. Have you ever tried to ignite a piece of paper with a magnifying glass? You try to get the sharpest, pinpoint image of the sun on the paper. Once you achieve that, Poof! the paper bursts into flames. The same occurs with hypnosis. When you focus your concentration to such a pinpoint degree, you become capable of accomplishments that far exceed any attempt you could possibly make using the diffuse focus of normal consciousness.

Conscious focusing is achieved in a hypnosis "script" by such phrases as "Listen only to the sound of my voice . . ." or "breathing regularly and deeply . . . regularly and deeply. . . ." Such devices are geared to narrow your focus and wean you away from your world of distractions. The intention is to focus your mind with a suggestion that eventually you are willing to accept beyond all doubt.

I realize that, for many people, their first exposure to hypnosis raises a host of mystical, magical, and, unfortunately, frightening expectations. Perhaps you will need to read through your script, or if you are particularly insecure, listen to your tape several times before you will recognize that hypnosis is merely a natural focusing of your own energy and intent. If you persist in listening to your hypnosis script, you will be introduced to a psychic potential that already exists within you. We are not creating anything or conjuring up anything here. Think of it as being introduced to a hidden talent that you already have but have been completely unaware of.

Aside from hypnosis' more obvious benefits, such as focus,

channeling of energy and will, concentration, and so on, hypnosis also serves as an affirmation of your positive intentions. It will keep you connected to your ego's ultimate desire for legitimate self-control and self-respect. Hypnosis will put you and your program of habit re-formation into gear. It will sustain the momentum of your Directed Imagination and fortify your resolve to succeed. The very essence of hypnosis is to awaken you to the vast potential that lies at your disposal, the potential to define the habit-free life you want to live.

In this chapter you will be given specific instructions for making a hypnosis tape recording appropriate to your addiction or habit. There is no doubt that having a hypnotist deliver the script is a distinct advantage in creating a suggestive ambiance (recall the effect Mesmer's flowing silk robes had on his patients). You, however, will find all the authority you need in the script itself and in the presentation of ideas. As long as you approach your hypnosis in a legitimate, cooperative spirit and give it adequate time and practice, you will be successful. You will not even miss the flowing silk robes.

How will you evaluate your hypnotic success? First of all, do not expect to lose consciousness, experience any mystical transportation, or have some other out-of-body experience. You are not going to feel any sort of altered consciousness during your hypnosis. In fact, the only thing you are likely to feel is more relaxed after the experience.

There are three criteria for evaluating your progress. They are: (1) learning to let go and to stop your rational intellect from making judgments during the process, (2) learning to follow the stated instructions to the best of your ability, and (3) learning to relax and focus your concentration on the script. Ultimately, however, your success will be measured by only one goal: the ability to live your life making appropriate choices, not the pseudo-choices born out of compulsive habit.

The Circle

The circle is a product of nature that has always held a special place in the human mind. From the prehistoric sun wheel to the alchemists' *rotundum,* the circle has played a major role in the religious and spiritual symbolism of our psychic development. The intricate and fascinating mandalas (the Sanskrit word for "circle") of the Tibetan lamas are awe-inspiring examples of this symbolism used for meditational practice and spiritual fulfillment. Nowhere is this mandala symbolism more beautifully expressed than in the stained glass windows adorning medieval cathedrals.

What is it about the circle that has inspired such universal appeal? Why has the circle been such a central symbol in religious expression, meditation, and introspection?

The circle is both the symbol and experience of order, totality, and perfection. For this reason it has historically been connected with various deities. Visually the circle conveys closure and completion. Psychologically it expresses containment, protection, and security. Its perfection and symmetry draw us into its center, and it embraces our fragmented lives. Swiss psychiatrist Carl Jung noted that the circle is often produced in the dreams of a person who is experiencing a kind of psychic fragmentation. The circle, he contended, occurs as a compensatory symbol, attempting to bind together or unify the psyche.

I recall my own experience of working with a young woman who was feeling dangerously fragmented. Her thoughts were becoming more and more chaotic and depressed. She spontaneously decided to paint a circular piece of plywood that had been lying in her garage. She began at the center and painted a yellow-white sun. Radiating out from the sun, she drew eight lines, like the spokes of a wheel. Within the first pie-shaped area, she painted a stormy sky with dark, menacing clouds and lightning spewing forth, followed in the next section by a sunny sky with white puffy clouds. The sections alternated — stormy sky, clear sky —going right around. As she progressed from the center to the circumference of the circle the skies gave way to what appeared to be the star-studded celestial sphere, the heavens. If you imagine a bicycle wheel, the space between the spokes contained the clear and stormy skies. The bicycle tire was the space where the heavens were painted. The tire tread, or the outer rim of the circle, was painted green, like grass, representing a return to terra firma.

She presented the mandala to me when she was finished. Working on it day by day, she had begun to feel more pulled together:

> *At first I just felt calmer. . . . But as the days progressed, I realized my circle had to be completed. . . . I wanted to stay in the center because it felt safe . . . secure . . . but I knew I had to return. It seemed that all of life's conflicts were portrayed in my stormy skies. Once I finished the clear skies, things began to feel more balanced. . . . You know, it wasn't all bad. . . . I had to understand this balance. . . . This was very important for me. The starry sky just sort of happened. . . . It gave everything a sort of tranquil feeling, you know like our, or my, place in the universe. Finally I had to finish my wheel. I painted the grass. . . . I was back from my journey.*

She did avoid a psychic breakdown. In fact the mandala symbolized a journey into her center and then back out again. Her healing energy had been harnessed through painting the mandala.

I have long felt that the symbol of the circle has tremendous healing as well as unifying capabilities. It can embrace you in calm when chaos looms all about you. For this reason I have used the circle as a focal point in these hypnosis scripts. In the "induction" portion of your hypnosis script (the part that helps you enter into a relaxed state), you will be asked to visualize a "large white circle drawn on a black background." Holding this image in your mind, you will be passively embraced by a sense of wholeness and serenity. You will be instructed to write and then erase numbers within this circle, all the time remaining involved and absorbed in the circle.

When you proceed to the "suggestion" portion of your script (the part that reinforces your desire to let go of your addiction, compulsion, phobia, or habit), the circle is again mentioned, this time as a tool for handling chaos. You will be told that whenever you face temptation, cravings, or discomfort, you are immediately to visualize the "large white circle," to allow it to "leap into your mind." The intention is to give you a reflexive way of bathing yourself with the mental imagery of the circle whenever you face fragmentation. The hypnosis acts to implant the suggestion that your circle can pop into your mind whenever you need help or protection. Once the circle is called to mind, you will be instructed to follow your breathing, in and out, in and out.

Not only does this technique distract you from your Beast, Spoiled Child, or Insecure Child, it also surrounds you with an experience of serenity. This technique is as ancient as the human species. Certainly the format used in hypnosis is very different from the meditational practices of the Tibetan monks or the religious experience one feels in viewing the rose window of the Cathedral of Notre Dame in Paris, but I assure you the circle holds the same capacity to soothe, comfort, and heal — regardless of how it is employed.

You will be instructed to use this technique whenever a craving or discomfort occurs. Remember that practice not only in relaxation and hypnosis but also in your circle meditation is essential if you expect to truly protect yourself from the manipulations of your internal characters.

Preparing Your Tape*

You will need a tape recorder and a high-quality 90-minute tape (45 minutes on each side). Before beginning to record your hypnosis tape (from the "induction" and "suggestion" scripts found later in this chapter), read through the material several times to get a feel for delivery. Initially, record only the induction script onto your tape. Read in a soft and relaxed voice. Make sure you keep your mouth close to the microphone throughout the recording to maintain proper volume. There is nothing less intimate than listening to a voice that sounds as if it were coming from down the street.

Keep in mind that any extraneous noise can be not only annoying but also anticipated whenever you listen to the tape. Such anticipation might wind up being a major distraction that could easily prevent you from having total concentration. If, for example, fifteen minutes into the taping you inadvertently sneeze, you may well spend the first half of every listening session thinking: "Here comes the sneeze.... Any second now...."

If you do happen to mess up and need to start the recording again, be patient. The end result will justify all of your efforts. The added practice of starting again will work to improve your delivery.

---

*If you do not wish to prepare your own tape, a high-quality hypnosis tape *Healing Your Habits*, narrated by Dr. Luciani, is available from LuraMedia Post Office Box 261668, San Diego, CA 92126.

Minimize recording problems by finding a small quiet room in which to do your recording (closets work very well). Of course, if you have a high-quality microphone, you have very little to worry about. Most tape recorders, however, with their little built-in omnidirectional microphones, present a bit of a challenge since they are designed to pick up noise from all directions, not just sounds that are in front of them. If you live in a particularly noisy neighborhood, you are better off making your recording late at night or early in the morning when there is less traffic, plane, and people noise.

Begin by speaking in a normal, clear, energetic voice. Slowly, paragraph by paragraph, allow yourself to slow down the delivery as you read through the text. Let your voice reflect the suggestion. Try to sound relaxed, soothing, and calm. To help you do this, I have used slash marks (/) wherever you need to pause. Each slash should equal about a one-second delay. For example, if you were to read "Your arms are heavy / / /" the three slash marks would indicate about a three-second delay.

It really helps to think about what you are reading as you speak. If you are oblivious to what you are reading, you will miss some nice, subtle inflections. So in the example above, when you record "Your arms are heavy / / /" feel your arms go heavy as you say the words. Whenever I hypnotize someone in my office, I try to hear my own voice as I speak and try to experience each suggestion as I read. This also helps you with your timing and will prevent you from rushing through the suggestion.

With a little practice, you will find that your delivery can improve dramatically. The best thing to do is to go ahead and record a paragraph or two, then listen to your delivery. You will sense where you need to change. If, on the other hand, you have a friend who is a bit theatrical, you might consider enlisting his or her help for the task. But please remember, it is the script that is important. The delivery is just the messenger. The words are the power.

Induction Script

Record this first section onto a 90-minute tape (45 minutes per side) so that you will not have to flip the tape over while you are listening to it. The second section, the "suggestion," will be added later.

[Begin recording:]
Find a comfortable position / uncross your legs and allow your arms to go heavy and loose at your sides / make sure your head is well supported / begin to allow your body to become more peaceful / more quiet / it is important for you to realize that another word for hypnosis is "cooperation" / as long as you allow yourself to cooperate, you will have success / / sometimes there is a tendency to fight or resist certain suggestions / don't be concerned / just gently guide yourself back and continue wherever you pick up the suggestion / should you hear a distracting sound or have a distracting thought / again / don't be concerned / just guide yourself gently back and follow my instructions to the best of your ability / you will remain conscious of all that takes place during this session and will have no trouble recalling the entire relaxed, peaceful experience afterward and throughout the day / / /

Should there be any urgent reason to wake during the session, you can just open your eyes and feel fully alert and mobile / /

Listen carefully to what I say / close your eyes / your eyes are closed / / you are feeling comfortable / / relaxed / / thinking of nothing / / nothing but what I say / / your eyes are closed / comfortably closed / you are thinking of nothing / / nothing but what I say / / / your arms and legs begin to feel heavy / / your arms and legs feel heavy and relaxed / / / relaxed / / / your whole body begins to feel more relaxed / / / your whole body begins to feel more relaxed / / / more and more relaxed / / / the muscles of your face / neck / and shoulders become relaxed / / your arms / your legs / relaxed / your whole body is relaxed /// you are listening only to my voice // only to my voice // thinking of nothing /// absolutely nothing //// concentrating only on my voice /// listening only to what I say // you are feeling comfortable and relaxed /// all the muscles in your body are relaxed // comfortable and relaxed /// as you let go of your thoughts, you also let go of your body // you let go and begin to drift // drifting into a drowsy / relaxed place // a drowsy relaxed place //// drowsy //// and relaxed //// you are thinking of nothing /// nothing but the sound of my voice /// you feel comfortable and relaxed /// comfortable and relaxed /// comfortable and relaxed //// breathing regularly and deeply //// regularly and deeply //// regularly and deeply //// thinking of nothing // nothing but the sound of my voice /// your breathing is regular and deep /// regular and deep /// deep /// deeper //// you let go and allow yourself to slip into a drowsy and relaxed place /// breathing regularly and deeply //// regularly and deeply //// regularly and deeply //// you allow yourself to slip more and more into your relaxation /// deeper and deeper into your relaxation /// deeper /// deeper //// relax //// relax ////

You feel comfortable and relaxed /// just letting go /// letting go /// listening only to my voice /// breathing regularly and deeply /// regularly and deeply /// going into a deep / sound relaxation /// drifting down / down // down // way down ///// breathing regularly and deeply /// regularly and deeply /// regularly and deeply /// take the next few moments to increase your relaxation / just be with the quiet and stillness // be aware only of your gentle and regular breathing as you let go of all tension and allow yourself to relax more and more // begin ... *[pause for about 30 seconds.]*

Now let's increase the feelings of relaxation / picture numbers as if they were written on a blackboard / one at a time / beginning with 1 and going up to 3 /// each number will increase your sense of relaxation and letting go // each number will increase the gentle / heavy / deeper feelings that you give into // picture a blackboard with a large white

CHANGING YOUR FOCUS ■ 113

circle drawn on it // imagine yourself drawing the number 1 in the center of the circle //// now erase this number carefully //// then write the word "relax" off to the side //// feel a growing sense of heaviness and calm // a nice, together feeling, as you allow yourself to slip deeper and deeper into the quiet part of your mind that allows you to relax /// allows you to relax /// allows you to let go and relax /// relax /// now imagine yourself drawing the number 2 in the center of the circle //// erase this number carefully //// write the word "relax" off to the side //// allow your heavy sensations to increase // feel your arms // heavy /// relaxed /// your legs // heavy /// relaxed /// relaxed //// limp //// as you continue to let go and drift down // down /// down //// into a drowsy relaxation /// a deeper relaxation than before /// much deeper /// much deeper //// much deeper ///// draw the number 3 in the circle // carefully erase it //// write the word "relax" off to the side ///// you may feel so loose and still and relaxed that your body feels as if it's floating // a free feeling // a feeling of release // just LETTING GO /// letting go and floating /// your arms are relaxed /// relaxed /// legs relaxed /// your breathing is relaxed and regular /// relaxed /// you grow more drowsy / more relaxed /// always going deeper // deeper /// deeper //// deeper //// every second that passes you find yourself giving up all tension and anxiety // listening only to my suggestions // without effort // relax and go deeper /// relax and go deeper //// relax //// relax //// relax ////

    In your mind's eye, imagine that you are going over to a window / you look outside // you see a large pine tree in the distance // beyond the tree you see a high sand dune // you notice clumps of sand grass moving in the gentle breeze // off in the distance beyond the dune is the ocean // you begin to walk toward the ocean // as you approach it you feel very calm and relaxed // not a care in the world /// as you approach the dune you see the shrubs and wild flowers there // you begin to climb the dune / feeling your feet give and sink in the warm sand // you climb higher / higher // you begin to get tired // pleasantly tired /// so tired //// finally you reach the top // from here you look out over the ocean // the powerful / rhythmic pattern of waves crashing into the surf // the blue sky // white puffy clouds drifting by /// you decide to lie down and relax a while /// to stretch out and relax a while /// you lie in the sun-heated sand // feeling your body melt as it displaces the warm sand /// you feel the sun warming you from above // you enjoy being sandwiched in this glowing, radiant warmth /// allow the warmth to flow through your body //// your hands /// your feet /// the warmth spreads into your legs /// your arms /// melting your muscles /// melting your muscles /// your face /// your neck /// you look up at the sky / white fleecy clouds slowly drift by // as you watch the clouds you allow yourself to relax more / and more // the changing moving shapes of the clouds allow you to go deeper // deeper // relaxing /// listening only to my voice // letting go of all thoughts /// allowing your consciousness to drift down // and down // way down . . . *[pause for about 15 seconds.]*

[End the induction recording here.]

Practice

Prior to your cessation date, listen to the induction portion of the tape at least once a day for three days (more if you have the time or feel that you are strongly resisting the hypnosis). The purpose of the induction is to relax you, both physically and mentally, getting you to focus your concentration in preparation for the suggestion that follows. Using the relaxation exercises contained in this section of the script will give you all the practice you need leading up to your target date.

Before sitting down to a practice session, make sure to arrange for an uninterrupted half hour. Try not to schedule your practice time too near bedtime. If you fall asleep, that is okay, but you will not digest the practice needed. Find a comfortable place to lie down with your head firmly supported. Remove any restrictive jewelry or tight clothing — glasses, belts, or the like. Unplug the phone and instruct everyone in the house to keep away.

Deep relaxation is essential in hypnosis. Thus, you should only listen to this tape in a quiet setting where distractions will be minimal. You should *not* listen to this tape while driving a car or operating any machinery. There is always the possibility that you may fall asleep.

Suggestion Scripts

After you have had some experience with your induction tape and feel that you are able to follow the instructions to the best of your ability, achieving a substantial degree of relaxation, then you are ready to move on to recording the suggestion portion of the tape appropriate to your addiction or habit: Smoking (p. 115); Compulsive Eating (p. 118); General Habit Control (to be used for phobias, obsessive thinking, general compulsions, or compulsive gambling) (p. 121); Alcohol and Drug Addiction (p. 124).

Suggestion Script for Smoking

[Begin Recording:]
   As you follow your slow, easy breathing / you become aware of clean fresh air entering your lungs with each inhalation / and nicotine waste leaving with every exhalation // as your lungs begin to repair the damage / moment by moment // breath by breath // you become aware that you are no longer a smoker // you repeat the words to yourself: "I AM NO LONGER A SMOKER!" /// One battle is now over / your decision to quit has been made // finally // after all this time // after feeling out of control // weak // addicted // finally you take your life back /// as you relax / taking in clean / fresh cleansing air / exhaling nicotine waste // you realize how good it feels to take charge of your own life // how powerful you feel at this moment /// you begin to experience this powerful / potent feeling /// staying relaxed /// relaxed //// allowing your body and mind to drift /// absorbing all my suggestions like a dry sponge /// you realize you can't go on living out of control // heaping up negative feelings // you

realize that now you can take charge of your life // finally ///
after all this time /// after all this struggle /// you finally take
control of your own life /// finally //// how good it feels ////
how powerful //// whenever you encounter an urge to smoke
/ weakness / or temptation / you will immediately / like a flash
/ see a large white circle drawn against a black background //
this circle will just leap into your mind whenever you experience an urge to smoke // once you see your circle, you will
slowly / in your mind / write the word "No" / just two large letters within the circle // N / O / and you will firmly say the
word "No" to yourself // if the urge is strong / you will / in
your mind / scream the word "No!" // see yourself screaming
the word "No!" at the top of your lungs /// "No!" to temptation / "No!" to the Spoiled Child within you that insists you're
too weak // "No!" to the Beastly cravings // you take charge
and decide to get tough with temptation // once you write
the word "No" in the circle, you then focus your mind on the
clean / cleansing air as it enters your mouth // follow this air
down your throat // actually see it /// feel it /// experience it
as it enters your lungs /// now follow this same breath as
nicotine waste is transported out of your lungs with your
exhalation /// continue to follow your breath / in /// and follow your breath / out /// in /// out /// continue to focus on
your breathing until the urge to smoke leaves you /// until
the urge leaves you /// until the urge is gone /// staying
focused on your breathing /// nothing else /// the more you
practice this method of total focus, the better you will get //
the more you practice, the better you will get // the stronger
you will become // the more confident you will become //
each and every urge will pass // the urges will pass /// finally
you take a stand against this indulgent / Spoiled / panicked
Child within you, and you say "No" // you scream the word
"No!" /// your life cannot be lived in any other way // you
can't be bullied any longer // now you do what you have to
do // you fight each urge // one at a time / and you defeat
each urge / one at a time /// how positive you feel /// imagine your hands / clean // uncluttered // no smoldering
cigarette // imagine your clothes smelling clean / fresh //

CHANGING YOUR FOCUS ■ 117

your hair / fingers / clean and fresh // no longer cradling a filthy ashtray / now you are free // in control // finally /// finally free //// you realize you need not live your life out of control ever again // this is it /// the end of weakness // the ability to say "No" // whenever you are confronted with an urge to smoke, you allow your white circle to flash into your mind like a bolt of lightning // you allow this to happen // you allow this to happen every time you are confronted with a temptation to smoke // and you slowly write the word "No" in the center of the circle / slowly / with patience / you write the word "No" // if the urge persists / you next focus your mind on your breathing / see your breath as it enters your mouth / follow this air down your throat / actually allow yourself to see it // to feel it // to experience it as it enters your lungs // allow this clean fresh air to scour your lungs / now free of nicotine // slowly follow the same breath as it leaves your lungs with your exhalation /// continue to follow your breath / in /// follow your breath / out /// in /// out /// continue to focus on your breathing until all temptation leaves you // until all temptation leaves you /// until all temptation is gone /// allow all your consciousness to be totally absorbed by your breathing // without thought // without reflection /// relax /// relax //// the more you practice this method of total focus, the better you will get // the more you practice, the better you will become at resisting temptation // the stronger you will become // the more confident you will become /// continue letting go and drifting down // and down /// way down now //// allowing your deep // deep / relaxation to return *[pause for 30 seconds.]*

You absorb all these suggestions easily / they become a permanent part of you /// a permanent part of you *[pause for 15 seconds]*

I'm going to count to three / as I count you will slowly begin to wake // like a bubble on the bottom of a lake you will slowly allow yourself to rise toward the surface // 1. /// quiet and relaxed /// feeling confident and powerful /// you begin to become aware of your body now //// you may feel like stretching a bit *[pause for 15 seconds.]* 2. // you begin to

become aware of your surroundings as you feel your normal wakefulness emerging / / your breathing becomes more normal as you continue to emerge from your relaxation / / /
3. / feeling well / awake / alert / as if you've had a restful nap / all tension and anxiety are gone / a complete sense of well-being and confidence becomes evident as you begin to stir.

You may open your eyes at any time / stay quiet for a while until you feel awake and alert.

[Pause for 15 seconds, then stop recording.]

Suggestion Script for Compulsive Eating

[Begin recording:]

As you allow yourself to drift / I would like you to imagine a large full-length mirror / create this mirror in your mind / see yourself / as you appear today / / look at your reflection / / / observe every detail / / / / try not to judge or react to what you see / / just record your image / / / / now turn the mirror around / / what you see on the reverse side of the mirror is a person who is lean, healthy, vital, and energetic / / the person you want to be / / living the life you want to live / free of compulsions / / just observe this reflection / / / / allow yourself to take a mental photograph of what you see / / / holding this image in your mind, begin to allow yourself to react to what you see / / react to this new / lean / athletic / energetic person you see in the mirror / / allow your good feelings to emerge / / how confident you look / / how powerful you feel at this moment / / / you begin to experience this powerful / potent feeling / / / staying relaxed / / / relaxed / / / / allowing your body and mind to drift / / / absorbing all my suggestions like a dry sponge / / / you begin to realize how out of control your life has been / / how the Child within you has ruled your life / / turn the mirror around again and see yourself as you are today / realize what your body reflects / / it reflects a willingness to be ruled by Beastly cravings / / to be manipulated by your inner Child / / your body reflects your choice to live with weakness / with doubt / to use food to handle life's difficulties // now turn the mirror around / see your new self / your new body // a body that reflects success / self-control / health / vitality // you need not go on living out of control / heaping up negative feelings //

Now you can take charge of your life / finally // after all this time // after all this struggle // you are finally taking control of your own life // finally /// you can finally say those words, "I WILL NO LONGER EAT COMPULSIVELY!" /// how good it feels /// how powerful /// whenever you encounter a feeling of weakness / a craving / a temptation / you will immediately / like a flash / see a large white circle drawn against a black background // this circle will just leap into your mind whenever you experience a temptation to eat what is wrong for you // once you see your circle / you will slowly / in your mind / write the word "No" / just two large letters within the circle / N / O / and you will firmly say the word "No" to yourself // if the urge is strong // in your mind / scream the word "No!" to yourself // see yourself screaming the word "No!" at the top of your lungs // "No!" to your temptation / "No!" to the Spoiled Child within you that insists you are too weak / "No!" to the Beastly urges that have dragged you around for so long // whenever you need to calm your mind / to strengthen your mind / you will immediately allow your mental photograph of your healthy, slim, energetic, body to fill your mind // seeing only this image / you will decide to ride out any temptation // all temptations will pass // the temptations will pass /// as the minutes tick away during a temptation, you begin to experience feeling powerful and in control // allow yourself to feel your strength // finally you are there //// finally you stand against this indulgent Child within you / and say "No" /// your life cannot be lived any other way / you cannot go on being bullied // whenever you're confronted with a temptation, you allow your white circle to flash into your mind like a bolt of lightning // you allow this to happen // you allow this to happen every time you are confronted with a temptation to eat the wrong kind of food / or too much food // you slowly write the word "No" in the center of the circle / slowly / with patience / you write the word "No" //

if your temptation persists / you focus your mind on your breathing / see your breath as it enters your mouth / follow this air down your throat // actually allow yourself to see it // to feel it // to experience it as it enters your lungs // feel your chest expand // now slowly follow the same breath as it leaves your lungs with your exhalation /// continue to follow your breath / in /// follow your breath / out /// in /// out /// continue to focus on your breathing until all temptation leaves you // until all temptation leaves you // until all temptation is gone /// staying focused on your breathing // thinking of nothing else // only your breathing // nothing else //// the more you practice this method of total focus, the better you will get // the more you practice, the better you will become at resisting temptation // the stronger you will become // the more confident you will become // finally you are taking charge of your own life /// how nice this feels // recall the mental photograph of the new you that you took standing in front of the mirror /// the lean / vital / healthy person you are meant to be // experience the positive feelings you feel every time you see yourself the way you are going to be /// at any point during the day you can refer to this mental photograph // use it to feel better // to give you strength // to encourage you //// allow yourself to continue to relax // relax /// feeling confidence surge through your body // your strength to say "No" // your strength to demand the quality of life you want to have // finally you are there /// relax //// relax //// continue letting go and drifting down //// and down //// way down now / allowing your deep / deep relaxation to return *[pause for 30 seconds.]*

    You absorb all these suggestions easily / they become a permanent part of you / a permanent part of you *[pause for 15 seconds.]*

    I am going to count to three / as I count you will slowly begin to wake and rise toward the surface / like a bubble on the bottom of a lake as it slowly drifts toward the surface // 1. // quiet and relaxed / feeling confident and powerful // you begin to become aware of your body now //// you may feel like stretching a bit *[pause for 15 seconds.]* 2. / you begin to become aware of your surroundings as you feel your normal wakefulness emerging / / your breathing becomes more normal as you continue to emerge from your relaxation / / / 3. / feeling well / awake / alert / as if you've had a restful nap / / all tension and anxiety are gone / a complete sense of well-being and confidence becomes evident as you begin to stir.

You may open your eyes at any time / stay quiet for a while until you feel awake and alert.

[Pause 15 seconds, and then stop recording.]

Suggestion Script for General Habit Control

If you choose, you may insert your particular habit (e.g., phobia, obsessive thinking, compulsive gambling, shopping, nail biting, fear of flying, etc.) in place of the word "habit" wherever it occurs in the script.

[Begin recording:]

As you allow yourself to drift / following your slow, easy breathing / allow yourself to recognize that you are no longer controlled by *[your habit]* / / / repeat the words to yourself "I AM NO LONGER CONTROLLED BY *[MY HABIT]*!" / / one battle is over now / your decision has been finalized / finally / after all this time / after feeling out of control / weak / addicted / / finally you are taking your life back / / / as you relax / allowing your breath to become more regular and deep / / / more regular and deep / / / you realize how good it feels to take charge of your own life / / how powerful you feel at this moment / / / begin to experience this powerful / potent feeling / / staying relaxed / relaxed / / / allowing your body and mind to drift / / to float / / / absorbing all my suggestions like a dry sponge / / / / you realize you can't go on living out of control / / heaping up negative feelings / / / you realize that now you can take charge of your life / / finally / / / after all this time / / / after all this struggle / / / you finally take control of your own life / / finally / / / how good it feels / / how powerful / / / whenever you encounter an urge / a weakness / or a temptation / / you will immediately / like a flash / see a large white circle drawn against a black background // this circle will just leap into your mind whenever you experience a temptation to indulge in *[your habit]* // once you see your circle, you will slowly / in your mind / write the word "No" / just two large letters within the circle // N / O / and you will firmly say the word "No" to yourself // if the urge is strong // you will / in your mind / scream the word "No!" // see yourself screaming the word "No!" at the top of your lungs /// "No!" to temptation / "No!" to the Child within you that insists that you're too weak // "No!" to the Beastly urges that have dragged you around for so long // you take charge and decide to get tough with weakness //// whenever you're confronted with a temptation / you allow your white circle to flash into your consciousness like a bolt of lightning // you allow this to happen // you allow this to happen every time you are confronted with *[your habit]* // you write the word "No" in the center of the circle // slowly / with patience // you write the word "No!" // if your temptation persists / you then focus your mind on your breathing / see your breath as it enters your mouth /// follow this air down your throat /// actually see it in your mind /// feel it /// experience it as it enters your lungs /// feel your chest expand /// now slowly follow this same breath as it leaves your lungs with your exhalation /// continue to follow your breath / in /// and follow your breath / out /// in /// out /// continue to focus on your breathing until all temptation leaves you // until all temptation leaves you /// until all temptation is gone //// staying focused on your breathing // thinking of nothing else // only your breathing // nothing else //// the more you practice this method of total focus, the better you will get // the more you practice, the better you will get // the stronger you will become // the more confident you will become /// each and every temptation will pass // every temptation will pass /// finally you stand firm against this indulgent / panicked Child within you and you say "No" // you scream the word "No!" // your life cannot be lived in any other way // you cannot be bullied any longer // now you do what you have to do /// you fight each urge / each weakness

/ each temptation / one at a time / / and you defeat each urge / each weakness / each temptation / one at a time / / / how positive you feel / / / now you are free / / / in control / / / finally / / / finally free / / / you realize you can't live your life out of control ever again / / / this is it / / / the end of weakness / / the ability to say "No" / allow your white circle to flash into your mind like a bolt of lightning / / you allow this to happen / / you allow this to happen every time you are confronted with a temptation / / you slowly write the word "No" in the center of the circle / slowly / with patience / you write the word "No" / / if the urge persists you next focus your mind on your breathing / see your breath as it enters your mouth / follow this air down your throat / actually allow yourself to see it / / feel it / / experience it as it enters your lungs / / feel your chest expand / / now slowly follow the same breath as it leaves your lungs with your exhalation / / / continue to follow your breath / in / / / follow your breath / out / / / in / / / out / / / continue to focus on your breathing until all temptation leaves you / / until all temptation leaves you / / until all temptation is gone / / / until you experience complete freedom / / / / relax / / / / relax / / / / continue letting go and drifting down / / / / and down / / / / way down now / allowing your deep / deep relaxation to return *[pause for 30 seconds.]*

You absorb all of these suggestions easily / they become a permanent part of you / / / a permanent part of you *[pause for 15 seconds.]*

I am going to count to three / as I count, you will slowly begin to wake / / like a bubble on the bottom of a lake, you will slowly allow yourself to rise toward the surface / / 1. / / / quiet and relaxed / / / feeling confident and powerful / / / you begin to become aware of your body now / / / / you may feel like stretching a bit *[pause for 15 seconds.]* 2. / / you begin to become aware of your surroundings as you feel your normal wakefulness emerging / / your breathing becomes more normal as you continue to emerge from your relaxation / / / 3. / feeling well / awake / alert / as if you've had a restful nap / all tension and anxiety are gone / a complete sense of well-being and confidence becomes evident as you begin to stir.

You may open your eyes at any time / stay quiet for a while until you feel awake and alert.

[Pause 15 seconds and then stop recording.]

Suggestion Script for Alcohol and Drug Addiction

Insert your particular addiction (e.g., drinking, cocaine, marijuana, etc.) in place of the word "addiction" in the script below.

[Begin recording:]
As you allow yourself to drift / following your slow, easy breathing / allow yourself to recognize that you are no longer controlled by *[your addiction]* / / / you repeat the words to yourself "I AM NO LONGER CONTROLLED BY *[MY ADDICTION]*!" / / one battle is over now / your decision has been finalized / finally / after all this time / after feeling out of control / weak / addicted / / finally you take your life back / / / as you relax / allowing your breath to become more regular and deep / / / more regular and deep / / / you realize how good it feels to take charge of your own life / / how powerful you feel at this moment / / / begin to experience this powerful / potent feeling / / staying relaxed / relaxed / / / allowing your body and mind to drift / / to float / / / absorbing all my suggestions like a dry sponge / / / / you realize you cannot go on living out of control / / heaping up negative feelings / / / you realize that now you can take charge of your life / / finally / / / after all this time / / / after all this struggle / / / you finally take control of your own life / / finally / / / you can finally say the words / "I will no longer be controlled by *[my addiction]*" / / repeat these words to yourself / / / / how good it feels / / how powerful / / / whenever you encounter a craving / a weakness / a temptation / / you will immediately / like a flash / see a large white circle drawn against a black background / / this circle will just leap into your mind whenever you experience a temptation to indulge in *[your addiction]* / / once you see your circle, you will slowly / in your mind / write the word "No" / just two large

letters within the circle // N / O / and you will firmly say the word "No" to yourself // if the craving is strong // you will / in your mind / scream the word "No!" // see yourself screaming the word "No!" at the top of your lungs /// "No!" to temptation / "No!" to the Child within you that insists that you're too weak // "No!" to the Beastly urges that have dragged you around for so long // you take charge and decide to get tough with weakness //// whenever you're confronted with a temptation / allow your white circle to flash into your consciousness like a bolt of lightning // you allow this to happen // you allow this to happen every time you are confronted with your habit // you write the word "No" in the center of the circle // slowly /with patience // you write the word "No!" /// if your temptation persists / focus your mind on your breathing / see your breath as it enters your mouth /// follow this air down your throat /// actually see it in your mind /// feel it /// experience it as it enters your lungs /// feel your chest expand /// now slowly follow this same breath as it leaves your lungs with your exhalation /// continue to follow your breath / in /// and follow your breath / out /// in /// out /// continue to focus on your breathing until all temptation leaves you // until all temptation leaves you /// until all temptation is gone //// staying focused on your breathing // thinking of nothing else // only your breathing // nothing else //// the more you practice this method of total focus, the better you will get /// the more you practice, the better you will get /// the stronger you will become // the more confident you will become /// each and every temptation will pass // every temptation will pass /// finally you tame the Beast /// you refuse to become intimidated any longer // you say "No" // you scream the word "No!" // your life cannot be lived in any other way // you cannot be bullied any longer /// now you do what you have to do /// you fight each craving / each weakness / each temptation / one at a time /// and you defeat each craving / each weakness / each temptation / one at a time /// how positive you feel /// now you are free /// in control /// finally /// finally free /// you realize you cannot live your life out of control ever again /// this is it /// the end of weakness // the ability to say "No" / allow your white circle to flash into your mind like a bolt of lightning // you allow this to happen // you allow this to happen every time you are confronted with a temptation // you slowly write the word "No" in the center of the circle // slowly / with patience / you write the word "No" // if the urge persists / focus your mind on your breathing / see your breath as it enters your mouth / follow this air down your throat / actually allow yourself to see it // feel it // experience it as it enters your lungs // feel your chest expand // now slowly follow the same breath as it leaves your lungs with your exhalation /// continue to follow your breath / in /// follow your breath / out /// in /// out /// continue to focus on your breathing until all temptation leaves you // until all temptation leaves you // until all temptation is gone /// until you experience complete freedom //// relax //// relax //// continue letting go and drifting down //// and down //// way down now / allowing your deep / deep relaxation to return *[pause for 30 seconds.]*

You absorb all of these suggestions easily / they become a permanent part of you /// a permanent part of you *[pause for 15 seconds.]*

I am going to count to three / as I count, you will slowly begin to wake // like a bubble on the bottom of a lake you will slowly allow yourself to rise toward the surface // 1. /// quiet and relaxed /// feeling confident and powerful /// you begin to become aware of your body now //// you may feel like stretching a bit *[pause for 15 seconds.]* 2. // you begin to become aware of your surroundings as you feel your normal wakefulness emerging // your breathing becomes more normal as you continue to emerge from your relaxation /// 3. / feeling well / awake / alert / as if you've had a restful nap / all tension and anxiety are gone / a complete sense of well-being and confidence becomes evident as you begin to stir.

You may open your eyes at any time / stay quiet for a while until you feel awake and alert.

[Pause 15 seconds and then stop recording.]

Steps For Success

1 Practice the preliminary exercise suggested at the beginning of this chapter (i.e., allowing your right foot to become heavy).

2 Become familiar with the three criteria for evaluating hypnotic success:

A. Having the ability to let go and to stop your rational intellect from making judgments during the process.

B. Being able to follow the stated instructions to the best of your ability.

C. Learning to relax and focus your concentration on the script.

3 Because of the importance of the circle technique as used in the scripts, I would advise rereading the section on "The Circle." Once you become familiar with the use of the circle as introduced in your hypnosis script, you can use it anytime, not just in response to cravings. Whenever you need to calm down or to feel more centered, you simply bring to mind your circle and follow your breathing. For the purpose of deep relaxation, rather than writing the word "No" in the circle (which you are taught in the suggestion script to use when fighting a craving), you may, instead, use the circle as described in the induction script. Here you are instructed to draw the number 1 in the center of the circle, erase it, and write the word "relax" off to the side; then draw 2 in the circle, erase it, and write the word "relax" off to the side, etc. You can count to three and then repeat the numbers, or, if you prefer, you can simply keep counting.

Imagine yourself standing in line at the grocery store. You begin to feel a vague sense of apprehension and irritability. In your mind you visualize the large white circle against the black background. You see yourself drawing the number 1 in the center of the circle. You carefully erase it. Then you write the word "relax." Keep counting and writing "relax" until you feel more centered. At that point, begin to follow your breathing, in and out, in and out. Keep the circle in mind as you follow your breathing. Try to let go of distracting thoughts as you become more and more involved with your circle. That is all there is to it. You can employ this technique anywhere: standing in a line, sitting at work, or trying to fall asleep.

Whether you follow your breathing for one minute or ten minutes, it will help. Whenever you interrupt the anxiety process, when you break the back of negativity, you begin to return to a more normal and relaxed place.

4 Arrange for a tape recorder and a 90-minute tape. Follow the instructions concerning recording very carefully. Record the "Induction Script."

5 Practice listening to the induction script at least once a day for three days — or longer if you have the time and/or you feel resistant to hypnosis.

6 Record the "Suggestion Script" for your particular habit.

7 Find the Checklist in the next few pages that is appropriate for you and mark off the steps that you have accomplished. When your Checklist is complete, you are ready to begin cessation.

8 Use the complete hypnosis tape to initiate your cessation. Listening to your hypnosis tape regularly will help you combat your cravings and strengthen your resolve to confront your characters. It is a vital part of healing your habit.

CHECKLISTS

Smoking Checklist

Before your cessation date, you should accomplish the following:

____ Read the Preview.

____ Read Chapter 1, including the *Steps for Success*.

____ Share your intentions with your friends.

____ Make a list of your reasons for quitting.

____ Read Chapter 2, including the *Steps for Success*.

____ Become familiar with Directed Imagination and be able to recognize the voices of the Beast, the Insecure Child, and the Spoiled Child.

____ Begin to record your dialogues with them.

____ Read Chapter 3, including the *Steps for Success*.

____ Begin to get adequate rest.

____ Decide on an exercise program.

____ If you are overweight and over forty, consult a physician.

____ Gather a supply of food for preventive snacks, bottled water, and multivitamins with a vitamin C supplement.

____ Read Chapter 4, including the *Steps for Success*.

____ Choose a journal and pen.

____ Set up a structured format in your journal for the first four days of cessation (96 hours).

____ Decide on rewards for yourself and make arrangements for them.

____ Read Chapter 5, including the *Steps for Success*.

____ Record the "Induction Script."

____ Listen to the induction tape at least once a day for three days.

____ Record the "Suggestion Script for Smoking."

____ Read Chapter 6.

____ Reread Chapter 1 "Preparing to Stop," "C-Day," and the *Steps for Success*.

____ Take whatever steps are necessary to make the first four days of your cessation hassle-free.

Compulsive Eating Checklist

Before your cessation date, you should accomplish the following:

____ Read the Preview.
____ Read Chapter 1, including the *Steps for Success*.
____ Share your intentions with your friends.
____ Make a list of your reasons for quitting.
____ Find out about your local chapter of Overeaters Anonymous (they welcome people with all sorts of eating disorders) and arrange to attend a meeting before your cessation date.
____ Read Chapter 2, including the *Steps for Success*.
____ Become familiar with Directed Imagination and be able to recognize the voices of the Beast, the Insecure Child, and the Spoiled Child.
____ Begin to record your dialogues with them.
____ Read Chapter 3, including the *Steps for Success*.
____ Begin to get adequate rest.
____ Decide on an exercise program.
____ If you are overweight and over forty, consult a physician; if you are anorexic or bulimic, consult a professional who specializes in eating disorders.
____ Choose a sensible food plan.
____ Gather a supply of healthy and nutritious food, bottled water, and multivitamins with a vitamin C supplement.
____ Read Chapter 4, including the *Steps for Success*.
____ Choose a journal and pen.
____ Set up a structured format in your journal for the first four days of cessation (96 hours) — include space for recording everything that you eat.
____ Decide on rewards for yourself and make arrangements for them.
____ Read Chapter 5, including the *Steps for Success*.
____ Record the "Induction Script."
____ Listen to the induction tape at least once a day for three days.
____ Record the "Suggestion Script for Compulsive Eating."
____ Read Chapter 6.
____ Reread Chapter 1 "Preparing to Stop," "C-Day," and the *Steps for Success*.
____ Take whatever steps are necessary to make the first four days of your cessation hassle-free.

Phobias Checklist

Before your cessation date, you should accomplish the following:

_____ Read the Preview.
_____ Read Chapter 1, including the *Steps for Success*.
_____ Make a list of your reasons for quitting.
_____ Read Chapter 2, including the *Steps for Success*.
_____ Become familiar with Directed Imagination and be able to recognize the voices of the Insecure Child and the Spoiled Child.
_____ Begin to record your dialogues with them.
_____ Read Chapter 3, including the *Steps for Success*.
_____ Begin to get adequate rest.
_____ Decide on an exercise program.
_____ If you are overweight and over forty, consult a physician.
_____ Gather a supply of food for preventive snacks and perhaps some bottled water.
_____ Read Chapter 4, including the *Steps for Success*.
_____ Choose a journal and pen.
_____ Decide on rewards for yourself and make arrangements for them.
_____ Read Chapter 5, including the *Steps for Success*.
_____ Record the "Induction Script."
_____ Listen to the induction tape at least once a day for three days.
_____ Record the "Suggestion Script for General Habit Control."
_____ Read Chapter 6, including the *Steps for Success*.
_____ Reread Chapter 1 "Preparing to Stop," "C-Day," and the *Steps for Success*.
_____ Take whatever steps are necessary to make the first four days of your cessation hassle-free.

Obsessive Thinking Checklist

Before your cessation date, you should accomplish the following:
- ____ Read the Preview.
- ____ Read Chapter 1, including the *Steps for Success*.
- ____ Make a list of your reasons for quitting.
- ____ Read Chapter 2, including the *Steps for Success*.
- ____ Become familiar with Directed Imagination and be able to recognize the voices of the Insecure Child and the Spoiled Child.
- ____ Begin to record your dialogues with them.
- ____ Read Chapter 3, including the *Steps for Success*.
- ____ Begin to get adequate rest.
- ____ Decide on an exercise program.
- ____ If you are overweight and over forty, consult a physician.
- ____ Gather a supply of food for preventive snacks and perhaps some bottled water.
- ____ Read Chapter 4, including the *Steps for Success*.
- ____ Choose a journal and pen.
- ____ Decide on rewards for yourself and make arrangements for them.
- ____ Read Chapter 5, including the *Steps for Success*.
- ____ Record the "Induction Script."
- ____ Listen to the induction tape at least once a day for three days.
- ____ Record the "Suggestion Script for General Habit Control."
- ____ Read Chapter 6, including the *Steps for Success*.
- ____ Reread Chapter 1 "Preparing to Stop," "C-Day," and the *Steps for Success*.
- ____ Take whatever steps are necessary to make the first four days of your cessation hassle-free.

General Compulsions/ Compulsive Gambling Checklist

Before your cessation date, you should accomplish the following:

_____ Read the Preview.

_____ Read Chapter 1, including the *Steps for Success*.

_____ Make a list of your reasons for quitting.

_____ If you are quitting gambling, find out about Gamblers Anonymous and plan to attend a meeting on your cessation date.

_____ Read Chapter 2, including the *Steps for Success*.

_____ Become familiar with Directed Imagination and be able to recognize the voices of the Insecure Child and the Spoiled Child.

_____ Begin to record your dialogues with them.

_____ Read Chapter 3, including the *Steps for Success*.

_____ Begin to get adequate rest.

_____ Decide on an exercise program.

_____ If you are overweight and over forty, consult a physician.

_____ Gather a supply of food for preventive snacks and perhaps some bottled water.

_____ Read Chapter 4, including the *Steps for Success*.

_____ Choose a journal and pen.

_____ If you are quitting gambling or some other compulsion in which you expect a lot of anxiety and chaos during withdrawal, you may choose to set up a structured format in your journal for the first four days of cessation (96 hours).

_____ Decide on rewards for yourself and make arrangements for them.

_____ Read Chapter 5, including the *Steps for Success*.

_____ Record the "Induction Script."

_____ Listen to the induction tape at least once a day for three days.

_____ Record the "Suggestion Script for General Habit Control."

_____ Read Chapter 6.

_____ Reread Chapter 1 "Preparing to Stop," "C-Day," and the *Steps for Success*.

_____ Take whatever steps are necessary to make the first four days of your cessation hassle-free.

Drug Addiction Checklist

Before your cessation date, you should accomplish the following:

____ Read the Preview.
____ Read Chapter 1, including the *Steps for Success*.
____ Share your intentions with your friends.
____ Make a list of your reasons for quitting.
____ Find out about your local Narcotics Anonymous group and make plans to attend a meeting on your cessation date.
____ Read Chapter 2, including the *Steps for Success*.
____ Become familiar with Directed Imagination and be able to recognize the voices of the Beast, the Insecure Child, and the Spoiled Child.
____ Begin to record your dialogues with them.
____ Read Chapter 3, including the *Steps for Success*.
____ Begin to get adequate rest.
____ Decide on an exercise program.
____ If you are overweight and over forty, consult a physician.
____ Gather a supply of food for preventive snacks, bottled water, and multivitamins with a vitamin C supplement.
____ Read Chapter 4, including the *Steps for Success*.
____ Choose a journal and pen.
____ Set up a structured format in your journal for the first four days of cessation (96 hours).
____ Decide on rewards for yourself and make arrangements for them.
____ Read Chapter 5, including the *Steps for Success*.
____ Record the "Induction Script."
____ Listen to the induction tape at least once a day for three days.
____ Record the "Suggestion Script for Alcohol and Drug Addiction."
____ Read Chapter 6.
____ Reread Chapter 1 "Preparing to Stop," "C-Day," and the *Steps for Success*.
____ Take whatever steps are necessary to make the first four days of your cessation hassle-free.

Alcohol Addiction Checklist

Before your cessation date, you should accomplish the following:

____ Read the Preview.
____ Read Chapter 1, including the *Steps for Success*.
____ Share your intentions with your friends.
____ Make a list of your reasons for quitting.
____ Find out about your local Alcoholics Anonymous group and make plans to attend a meeting on your cessation date.
____ Read Chapter 2, including the *Steps for Success*.
____ Become familiar with Directed Imagination and be able to recognize the voices of the Beast, the Insecure Child, and the Spoiled Child.
____ Begin to record your dialogues with them.
____ Read Chapter 3, including the *Steps for Success*.
____ Begin to get adequate rest.
____ Decide on an exercise program.
____ If you are overweight and over forty, consult a physician.
____ Gather a supply of food for preventive snacks, bottled water, and multivitamins with a vitamin C supplement.
____ Read Chapter 4, including the *Steps for Success*.
____ Choose a journal and pen.
____ Set up a structured format in your journal for the first four days of cessation (96 hours).
____ Decide on rewards for yourself and make arrangements for them.
____ Read Chapter 5, including the *Steps for Success*.
____ Record the "Induction Script."
____ Listen to the induction tape at least once a day for three days.
____ Record the "Suggestion Script for Alcohol and Drug Addiction."
____ Read Chapter 6.
____ Reread Chapter 1 "Preparing to Stop," "C-Day," and the *Steps for Success*.
____ Take whatever steps are necessary to make the first four days of your cessation hassle-free.

6

ESTABLISHING A CONTEXT:
PSYCHOLOGICAL AUTOBIOGRAPHY

Structuring Your Personal Program

☐ **Smoking**
Although it is important to read through Chapter 6 prior to your cessation date, you will find that the psychological context is a tool you will learn to use after your cessation date. Pay particular attention to Bill's story. Read through the *Steps for Success*. They will guide you in writing your psychological autobiography. This should be done after you have weathered withdrawal.

☐ **Compulsive Eating**
Read through Chapter 6 and begin to consider the psychological roots of your compulsive behavior in regard to food. Study the *Steps for Success*. You may want to postpone writing your autobiography until after you have gotten through the initial stages of withdrawal (the *Steps for Success* will give you instructions).

☐ **Phobias**
Chapter 6 will help you begin to understand the psychological roots of your phobia. Pay attention to the *Steps for Success*. They will guide you in writing out your psychological autobiography.

☐ **Obsessive Thinking**
This chapter will be helpful in examining the psychological context of your obsessive thinking. Note especially Jane's story. The *Steps for Success* will guide you in writing out your psychological autobiography.

☐ **General Compulsions/Compulsive Gambling**
It is important to become familiar with the concepts in Chapter 6 before your cessation date, but the psychological context is a tool that you will learn to use after your cessation date. Study the *Steps for Success*, which will aid you in writing your psychological autobiography. Your autobiography can be written before or after you get through withdrawal.

☐ **Drug Addiction**
Read Chapter 6. The psychological context is a tool you will find increasingly helpful, once you weather the storm of withdrawal. The *Steps for Success* will help you write your psychological autobiography.

☐ **Alcohol Addiction**
Read Chapter 6. Understanding the psychological context of your addiction before your cessation date is important, but you will use the tool most effectively once you have gotten through the withdrawal experience. Pay attention to Bill's story. The *Steps for Success* will help you write your psychological autobiography.

Perhaps you have wondered why your addictive tendencies are so resistant to change. Whenever you have attempted in the past to realign your thinking and break away from these destructive patterns, things have always gotten monstrously confusing. A primary reason for all this difficulty has to do with the fact that addictive behavior as well as habituated behavior and thinking is usually contaminated with remnants of some previous developmental difficulties. Such early difficulties, associated primarily with psychological woundedness, have a way of following you through life and ultimately finding a home in the destructive habits of the present.

Your life patterns today are both reflections of and reactions to your past. Obsessive or phobic worrying; compulsive behavior such as overeating, gambling, and nail biting; and even addictions to nicotine, alcohol, and drugs contain elements of past insecurities. I will be the first to acknowledge that there are people who break destructive habits every day without an inkling of insight into their past. Nevertheless, I would contend that only through an appreciation of the historical background of your habit will you find a more substantial and permanent cure.

Understanding the root of your problem will also reduce the possibility of habit substitution (e.g., that you will become an obsessive eater to compensate for your loss of cigarette smoking). Although a search for the origin of your difficulties may seem a somewhat arduous and elusive task, you will, nonetheless, be adequately prepared for it by using Directed Imagination, maintaining your journal, and following the suggestions in this chapter.

One additional tool that you will find very helpful in trying to establish connections between your past and the present is writing out your life story — writing a psychological autobiography. Although not an essential task in preparing for your planned cessation date, writing out your life story will prove indispensable in the days, weeks, and months that follow cessation. In fact, if you are to reach a more permanent healing, then a psychological autobiography is a vital part of your postcessation program.

In athletics, whether it is bowling, pitching a baseball, or throwing horseshoes, if you stop your body motion at the moment of release, you will never excel. Only when you learn to follow through — continuing your motion after the moment of release — will you gain mastery over your sport. Habit re-formation also requires follow-through at the moment of release from your habit. Anyone can throw a ball or a horseshoe, but only a few become masters of the game. Likewise, anyone can quit a habit, but how many can remain habit-free? Following through with your psychological autobiography will insure your ultimate victory.

Once you recognize that your addictive behavior evolved from yesterday's influences, you will be able finally to understand what your life needs to achieve balance. Initially, your addictive habits were attempts, albeit inappropriate, to meet these needs. They were nothing more than misguided attempts to plug the dike of insecurity, past disappointments, or psychic wounds. Once you can articulate clearly what your life needs now, as an adult, you can go about finding satisfaction and completion. Your addictive habit was (and still is) your Child's feeble attempt to find balance. What do you expect from a child?

I have selected two stories to illustrate the process of establishing this historical connection. Both people were involved in therapy while they were going through their habit re-formation. My comments and involvement in each case will help you to understand the type of thinking, pondering, and questioning necessary with your own material. My role as therapist clearly defines the role you want to adopt with yourself. Through your ongoing work with your journal, Directed Imagination, and your psychological autobiography, you will learn to become more impartial, objective, accepting, and intuitive about your own process. Like working on a connect-the-dot puzzle, you will make one connection after another until you begin to perceive the total picture.

The most obvious benefit of working with a flesh-and-blood therapist is the speed and efficiency of the process. You yourself, however, are quite capable of making the same connections and understanding the psychological context of your addiction.

The psychological context involves an understanding and appreciation of the total milieu, both present and historical, in which your habituated patterns operate. Each of the studies that follow reflects this complete approach to understanding addictive tendencies. In the *Steps for Success* at the end of this chapter you will be given detailed instructions for writing your psychological autobiography and for establishing your historical context. For now, just study these examples until you have a fundamental sense of how such connections are made from the past to the present. Only when you come to recognize where your internal characterizations of the Spoiled Child and the Insecure Child were born, can you come to appreciate the full range of their destructive involvement in your addictive behavior.

The examples I have selected may seem a bit extreme. For the sake of illustration, I felt it was more important to offer vivid symptoms and obvious background entanglements. Do not feel you need to relate to either person's specific difficulties. Just observe how the process of linking elements from the past with those in the present forms the psychological context. It should also become quite apparent to you from these accounts that the payoff for such demanding effort is nothing less than a complete and thorough liberation from addiction.

Jane: Liberation from Obsessive Worrying

Jane was a part-time bookkeeper and mother of two. She sought therapy because of chronic anxiety coupled with obsessive worries about getting cancer. Although she had experienced similar anxiety about sixteen years ago, it was not until the past three years that her anxiety became focused specifically on cancer and death.

She described her marriage as fulfilling and saw her husband as being very supportive throughout her ordeal. She would call him frequently at work (as she did her physician and me) just to have him tell her that she was not dying. Once assured that she did not have cancer and would be okay, she would feel relieved enough to go on for a while.

The assurance, however, never eliminated the worry. It just made it a bit more tolerable. I should point out that she called me least because I refused to tell her she was not dying. Instead, I insisted on getting her to focus on her panic, using Directed Imagination. I would ask her, for example, "Who is it in you that can't believe you're okay?" You may have already guessed that Jane did not really want to be asked such heavy questions. She would much rather have been told that everything was fine and that there was absolutely nothing to worry about.

Once I suggested that her husband come in and learn to become less codependent, less of an accessory to her anxiety. She refused to consider this on the grounds that it was better to depend on her husband to lower her anxiety than to be dependent on tranquilizers.

Initially in treatment Jane wanted only to talk about her symptoms, which seemed to roam week by week from headaches (brain tumors), to diarrhea (colon cancer), to thoughts of lung cancer (she was a heavy smoker). She originally came to therapy not at all convinced it was necessary but because her physician insisted. As far as she was concerned, her cancer had just not been detected as yet. She reminded me often that there was nothing psychological about her problem. You can imagine how she resisted my early attempts to get her to explore the symbolic relevance of her anxiety. Regardless of how much progress we would make during a session, she would always finish with the question, "Do you think I have cancer?"

From what you have learned about Directed Imagination, you should be able to detect the work of an Insecure Child in Jane's obsession with cancer. The first questions we asked in trying to establish the psychological context of Jane's problem were, "Who is asking everyone about cancer? Who needs some adult to tell her she is okay?"

Projection

The irony was that her husband — who had no medical expertise, no access to her tests, no clinical understanding of her condition — could soothe her just by saying, "Nothing's wrong." You would think the only calming voice would be that of her physician. With the Insecure Child, any "adult" can bring assurance as long as they carry the necessary projections once associated with "Mommy" or "Daddy."

Projection is an interesting, and for our purposes critical, defense mechanism. Just as a slide projector projects the image of a slide onto a screen, we can project our inner turmoil, needs, or fears onto various screens. These screens are often other people, as was the case with Jane. Incidentally, projection is an unconscious process, so do not think that you are going to be aware of these tendencies at first.

Jane would project (unconsciously) her parental associations onto her husband, her physician, and me. All three of us, through the mechanism of Jane's projection, possessed the power to "know" about her cancer. Perhaps even more importantly, the three of us all represented the capacity to liberate her from her worries. Projection is a very potent mechanism.

Young children typically (if not universally) project a godlike image onto their parents, who become nothing less than divine and omnipotent. Have you ever seen a toddler trip and fall, then get up, absolutely red-faced, and yell at his parent? Since parents are perceived as being godlike, they must have the power to prevent any evil. If the child comes to some ill, then the perception is that Mommy or Daddy must have allowed this to happen.

Projections can just as easily be connected with habits. Food, for example, may hold some magical projections about its capacity to remedy life's woes. Obsessive cleaning may represent a projected desire to gain control and mastery over a not-so-secure life. Unlike life, which becomes so complex, getting a room perfectly clean is an achievable task. It is a taste of what one seeks to experience from within, an approximation of where one wants to be — in control, balanced, and fulfilled.

As long as you project your heroes and demons outside yourself (projections can also be negative as is the case with jealousy, where you see the other person as one who can never be trusted), you remain limited in your ability to change. Only by reeling in your projections and recognizing their sources, do you begin to unravel the mystery of your obsessions and compulsions.

Jane the adult was emotionally no different from Jane the toddler because her projections kept her from maturing and recognizing her own psychological resources. She felt that her condition could be helped only if some adult-parent could convince her that nothing was wrong. Remember how she would leave our sessions, fishing for my omnipotence: "Do you think I have cancer?" No matter how much progress we made, when our session would end, the Insecure Child would begin to panic and insist on asking me if she were okay.

Using her journal, Jane discovered that her Insecure Child felt I was withholding my power from her. I was withholding power that could have made her whole. This left her Child feeling frustrated and angry with me. If only I would stop being so difficult and tell her what she needed to know. Then she could be cured.

In a way she was right. I did possess a kind of power to make her whole. But certainly not the power she was longing for. What I possessed was a strategy, a method of gaining perspective and freedom from her unconscious obsessions. Unfortunately, at this phase of her treatment, Jane was not interested in learning any method, strategy, or insight. She was not interested in taking any personal responsibility for her obsessive thinking and projections.

Overprotective Parents

After overcoming significant resistance, we were finally able to go beyond talking about Jane's physical complaints and look into her autobiographical account. Until this point her sessions had been a descriptive narrative of her pains and cancer fears. Once we began to look more symbolically at her fear and its history, we discovered, for starters, that both her parents had been overprotective, always shielding Jane from life's problems. She was never encouraged to work out her problems. Why should she? They did everything for her. In third grade she was teased because of her weight. Rather than help her lose weight (food was used medicinally in Jane's home to soothe life's rough spots) or help her deal with the teasing, they pulled her out of the public school and put her in a private school. I am convinced that if Jane had had difficulties with a neighborhood bully, her parents would have sold their home and moved!

When it came to growing up, the reins only became tighter. Her parents made a habit of removing offensive newspapers from the home to protect Jane from worrying about a war that was taking place in Europe. From her classmates she learned of a world she was totally unprepared to understand. Invariably, Jane wound up spending most of her time at home, where she felt more secure. Jane remembers being rather shy and introverted, only rarely having friends over to visit. Her parents always tried to compensate for her lonely life by giving her things at home: a swimming pool, stereo, television, and so on. The only tragedy, according to Jane, was that she had to grow up and become aware of her inadequacies.

With a little practice, Jane learned to suppress most of these inadequacies and fears and, for all intents and purposes, began to live a normal life. She married young, managed somehow to leave her parents' home, and apparently derived a great deal of pleasure from her children. Although she was generally happy during this period, she recalled having bouts of anxiety that seemed to occur for no particular reason (no conscious reason).

The more severe anxiety attacks began shortly after Jane moved East with her family, leaving her parents in California. She later experienced an intensification of symptoms when her own children began to approach adolescence and separate from her.

Jane eventually began to understand how the Insecure Child became such a dominating aspect of her psyche. At first she was reluctant to see this, primarily because this understanding made it necessary to shift from other-reliance to self-reliance. From this point it was a short leap to understanding that her fear of cancer was the Insecure Child saying, "I can't handle this world. There's too much pain, sickness, death."

Leaving the Garden

For Jane, cancer symbolized losing control. By its very nature, cancer represents a proliferation of cells — a machine gone wild. Jane's anxiety began to proliferate when she left her childhood home and the protection of her parents. She began looking for a special adult to take away the shadow side of the world. She wanted to say "No" to disease, pain, and suffering. She wanted absolute control over her life. Mythically, she only wanted the bliss connected with being back in the Garden of Eden. In a sense, she felt she was thrown out of the Garden prematurely, thrown out into the world of good and evil, a world of duality where pain, suffering, and death are all a part of life, a world for which she was totally unprepared.

From a psychological perspective, Jane's Insecure Child felt it was necessary somehow to get back into the Garden at all costs, back to a world where everything was controlled. As you and I know, once out of the Garden, no one returns. We cannot become an infant again and live in a blissful state of undifferentiated unconsciousness and total dependency. Getting Jane to take responsibility, through Directed Imagination, was, of course, demanding that she allow the Garden fantasy to die. Once she did accept my interpretations, she essentially was admitting that she could never return to Eden.

You can imagine how difficult this was for Jane. She actually began to experience a mild grief reaction. Giving up hope for the Garden must occur in every life if we are to progress and mature as adults. Usually this takes place during adolescence when our transition from childhood to adulthood is expected and encouraged. For Jane this transition was never accomplished, and only now, in the second half of her life, was she finally able to understand the regressive longings of her Insecure Child. Once she developed the capacity to figure out whatever the Child threw at her, her habit re-formation began to progress rapidly.

Relying on Her Own Resources

I encouraged her to stop calling her husband, physician, and therapist for assurance and, instead, to turn to her mature ego for solace. She did this, reluctantly at first, then with ever-increasing ease. On one level, cancer was a projection of Jane's profound distrust. She just could not believe that her body would stay healthy. After all, she had never had any practice in relying on her own resources. Why should her immune system be any easier to trust? Coming from a background where she had always been rescued and infantilized, she had no idea that, once deprived of her parents' magic, she could survive.

Whenever the Insecure Child would shrink from life, Jane learned to step in and declare: "I refuse to say 'No' to any aspect of life." She was not becoming a masochist, opening her arms to life's adversities. It was more a willingness to accept the inevitability of her fate, to accept life the way it is rather than to seek someone (a parent projection) to protect her magically from it.

Jane eventually acknowledged that her cancer obsession was a vehicle concocted by the Insecure Child's desire to avoid growing up and trusting her own resources. Cancer, unfortunately, is part of the real, adult world. Jane's Child wanted nothing to do with such terrifying realities. Once she recognized this, Jane was finally able to understand that her fears had nothing to do with cancer and everything to do with growing up, facing life, and believing in her capacity to take care of herself. From this point on, the tide of psychic battle shifted, and the Insecure Child was never seriously able to challenge Jane's mature ego position again.

Jane's journal offered her little help at first. Her early entries were merely a reflection of her symptoms (e.g., *This pain in my head seems to be getting worse. It's different from any headache I've ever had. I'm sure this is something unusual*). As her Directed Imagination became more and more established, she began to use her journal to get involved in the struggle between the rational ego and the irrational Insecure Child. Some of her battles were epic.

Hypnosis was definitely catalytic in allowing Jane to choose between irresponsibility and responsibility. Hypnosis (especially the technique of writing "No!" in the circle) also provided a structure for confronting the Child and taking a stand. Once she developed the ability to choose to go against the Insecure Child's intentions, a major victory was achieved in her treatment.

Establishing a historical context was the critical synthesizing element in Jane's habit re-formation and served to solidify her direction for the future. Recognizing her Child's projections, she came to understand her lifelong hesitancy to assume responsibility for her own life. Once the Insecure Child was thus exposed, Jane was in a very powerful position to negotiate her life choices.

Jane's program was an evolution of confidence, orchestrated from the very beginning by her Directed Imagination. Hypnosis, rest, exercise, diet, journal, and autobiography all played significant roles in her ultimate liberation.

If you were to talk to Jane today, she would tell you that she was once a child who never grew up, a child who tenaciously fought to return to the bliss and protection of her youth, a child convinced that growing up itself was a disease, offering nothing but misery. She would be eager to tell you that all these thoughts were bubbling, not in her conscious mind, but in the caldron of her unconscious, like thieves in the night robbing her of life. She knows better now. She has come to realize that the Garden is not what it is cracked up to be. Her choice is to live in the real world, not to hide from it.

Bill: Liberation from Smoking

Jane's case describes a psychological pattern where intrusive thoughts dominate and control life. Our second example is Bill, a man physically addicted to nicotine. Perhaps you have never considered looking at cigarette smoking as part of a total psychological pattern, but, again, I will remind you that human behavior never occurs in a vacuum. It is always wrapped in a shroud of associations and historical connections. Not everyone who tries a cigarette becomes addicted, not everyone yields to compulsions. Only when our psyche becomes receptive to habituated or addictive patterns do we become susceptible. This receptivity to compulsion is clearly demonstrated in Bill's account.

Bill is a rather intense man in his early forties. He had been smoking heavily since he was a freshman in high school. Bill describes himself as a "competitive guy" who "usually finds ways to succeed." He works as a high school gym teacher and finds his job very demanding. He is married with one child. His marriage was what I would describe as "undeveloped." Neither he nor his wife seemed eager to invest any energy into the relationship. Bill tended to be an extremist as a father — at one point showering his son (and his wife) with gifts and surprises, and then going for long periods without speaking to anyone.

When we started treatment, it was evident that Bill was looking for a magic bullet to stop smoking. He had been to a popular smoke-stop clinic in the area and had tried all the gimmicks he could find — gums, plastic cigarettes, and tapes — but all with no success.

When I began to explore with him the psychological context of his habit, Bill became resistant. He was not coming to me to be "analyzed," he declared. But in spite of his initial unwillingness, Bill became quite a talker.

One thing we learned from our very first meeting was that he saw himself as a "hoarder." As a child he remembered going to Saturday matinees at his neighborhood theater, Hershey bar in hand. While his friends wolfed down their snacks, Bill would meticulously dissect his chocolate bar into minute pieces, which he would then carefully ration to prevent running out during the movie. At home he would never eat a whole cupcake or piece of cake unless he was assured there would be some left for later.

It was not only food that Bill rationed. For instance, he would never play "too long" with one particular toy for fear of either wearing it out or breaking it. He described himself as being selfish, sensing that no one would protect his things as carefully as he would. To this day he has trouble letting his wife drive his car.

An Adult Child of an Alcoholic

Bill's father was an alcoholic who usually kept everyone in the house guessing whether violence would erupt when he got home. Having a volatile, alcoholic father probably affected Bill's sense of security more than any other experience. Certainly Bill's emptiness and inordinate need for protection can be directly traced to this anxiety source. Bill worked very hard at keeping a low profile, trying to stay out of harm's way while struggling to provide for his own needs.

Bill started working in his early teens. He found that having money gave him a sense of control over his roller-coaster life. Working allowed Bill to eat out regularly, avoiding the particularly difficult time at home in the evening when his father arrived. Whenever he ate out, he would always overorder, telling the server to add extra French fries or extra bread to his meal. It was not so much a need to binge as a feeling that he would never get enough. Perhaps more accurately stated, Bill was trying to avoid, and at the same time fill, his gnawing sense of emptiness. This began a pattern of weight gain that has persisted throughout his adult life.

Around the end of his thirteenth year, Bill began smoking. He remembered two reasons. One was to fit in with a certain high school crowd from which he felt excluded. The second reason was to try to compensate for his general embarrassment about having a delayed puberty. Whenever he put a cigarette to his lips, he felt "just as good as the next guy." Cigarettes became an immediate answer to Bill's already overwhelming insecurity, and, like everything else, he pursued his new habit excessively.

Smoking put him in the driver's seat, able to feel satisfied whenever he wanted to be. When he managed to have an ample supply of cigarettes on hand, he was a different person, more outgoing, friendly, and less moody. He was usually able to coerce his mother into buying him cigarettes by the carton when she went shopping. Interestingly enough, no one at home made a great fuss about a thirteen-year-old boy smoking! Having a whole carton of unopened cigarettes was a high that made him feel "on top of the world."

If it had not been for a girlfriend objecting, Bill would never have noticed a sort of "snapping" sound he made every time he pulled a cigarette from his sucking lips. Not only did he attack and devour each cigarette, but he would also smoke them right down to the filter, and then some. Bill became a heavy chain-smoker, sometimes smoking close to four packs of cigarettes a day. He had decided to quit (again) because of constant ridicule at work and a lingering morning cough.

Following the Program

Once Bill got acclimated to what he referred to as his "analysis," he eagerly agreed to follow my program. We set a target date and decided to continue our talks until that date. Bill had some initial difficulty with hypnosis and required a few practice sessions to learn to relax sufficiently. His only other resistance was to keeping a journal. He approached this part of the program with a negative mind-set. He felt that the journal was superfluous because, for him, he could just keep mental notes. He assured me he would not forget anything. Finally he yielded to my warnings that during nicotine withdrawal his thoughts would be anything but orderly and reliable. Fortunately, Bill had had plenty of experience to confirm this in his previous attempts at quitting.

I should point out that resistance is a typical defense seen in addictive and habituated patterns. If you expect the Spoiled Child to say, "I can't do that," "This is stupid," etc., then you will be prepared to put your foot down and insist on strict adherence to the program.

Once Bill reached his target date, I saw little of him for about three weeks, at which point he made an appointment. He came in smiling from ear to ear. He informed me that he had "made it." He had had a rather violent withdrawal at first but felt that his preventive snacking and rigid compliance with the program pulled him through.

His journal had no entries — just check marks — for the first three days. Then came a flurry of voluminous notes on his Beast struggles, a few choice words directed toward me and my program, and a few at his

Maker. His struggle was typified by the evolution of both the Insecure Child and the Spoiled Child along with the Beast. The physical manifestations of his addiction were represented by the Beast (cravings). The Spoiled Child was most evident in Bill's stubborn resistance and whining. It was, however, the Insecure Child who added a totally new dimension.

The Insecure Child

From this Child, Bill was able to connect with the elements of our previous "analysis" and to realize his patterns of insecurity. He saw his addiction to nicotine as one more manifestation of his protecting himself from the pain and emptiness brought about by an inadequate, wounded father. All the loose ends became bound together as Bill realized that his hoarding, eating, emotional volatility, and smoking (especially with the snapping/sucking sounds he used to make) were all attempts to rectify a need, a hunger, for emotional intimacy that had eluded him throughout his life.

Bill really became proficient with his Directed Imagination through the months of habit re-formation that followed. The psychological context that we had established provided Bill with a window through which he could peer to understand the connections that spanned his entire life. The Insecure Child ultimately became his constant antagonist, usually reflecting his turbulent insecurity, which was slowly beginning to yield to more moderate feelings of self-trust and self-esteem.

Bill and I have stayed in touch (in spite of his early resistance to "analysis") and now, after more than two years, Bill still uses his Directed Imagination often, particularly when he sees himself "hoarding for winter," as he puts it. He clearly understands that all his symptoms come from the same pit of insecurity. There had been only one purpose: to fill the emptiness, an emptiness Bill now takes full responsibility for filling.

He has been working very hard at his marriage, learning to trust the love around him. Recently he informed me that not only does he not dissect his Hershey bars anymore, but he willingly and lovingly offers a bite to anyone he is with.

Choose Expansion!

The primary emphasis of the first five chapters of this book has been to teach you to use Directed Imagination to gain control of destructive thought patterns that have become linked to addictive behavior. The structural elements of hypnosis, keeping a journal, rest, exercise, and diet are all ancillary components serving to enhance the implementation of this program. Once employed, Directed Imagination is capable of handling the confrontations with your addiction, compulsion, phobia, or obsession with predictable reliability.

For many, the healing of disturbing habits is where they choose to end their program. If, however, you choose to proceed with your efforts, to learn to follow through, being symptom-free becomes only the beginning, a catapult into a new dimension of living best described as a realization of life's propensity for expansion.

If you do choose expansion, then it is time for you to establish your psychological context. It involves a process of gathering the loose threads of your life and learning to weave them together to form a tapestry of meaning and relevance. From this tapestry you are able to glean the origin of your woundedness, which from the beginning has been generating defensive and compensatory behavior. Once you expose the wounds, you will understand what your inner Child truly seeks.

In Jane's case, an understanding of her psychological context allowed her to see that it was not cancer that moved her Child to hysteria. Her obsession was the Insecure Child's attempt to regress to the bliss of childhood dependency, where her ego development had become frozen. Bill's Child, at least on the surface, manifested itself primarily through smoking and eating. Only when the psychological context was established, did it become evident that these seemingly "normal" habits were imbued with the panic of an Insecure Child seeking to fill a gnawing emptiness that dated back to his early experiences with his alcoholic father. When you finally come to appreciate what you really need rather than what your inner Child needs, then you can begin to eliminate the addictive intrusions in your life.

Life demands only one thing from you: that you seek to express your nature. Just as the miraculously packaged acorn seeks its ultimate expression in the mighty oak, so too is your potential for individuation contained within your being. Thwart this potential and life will turn against you. Such has been the case with your addictive tendencies.

You must now choose either to pursue your nature or to continue wrestling with the contorted reactions of insecurity. If your choice is personal expansion, then you must learn to liberate yourself from your past. Learn this by scrutinizing your habits and confronting your Insecure Child and/or your Spoiled Child. Learn this by ultimately allowing and helping your Children to mature. The intent of Directed Imagination is not to kill, abandon, or orphan the Child. Rather the goal is to support, educate, love, and encourage mature living.

Directed Imagination promotes consciousness, the ability to know what is and what is not in your own best interest. You learn to say no to all that is inappropriate, maladaptive, and neurotic. Instead, you become capable of making life choices that reflect your true nature.

My words are finished now, as they should be. The process must now be turned over to you. Accept the responsibility for your life willingly. Do not be deceived by the Spoiled Child's insistence that you are not up to it. Everything you will ever need to succeed you already possess. Choose to believe it!

Steps For Success

1 The first step before beginning your autobiography is to identify the internal characterizations of your habit as outlined in Chapter 2 on Directed Imagination. After you have established "who" is doing your talking when conflicts arise, you will be ready to proceed to the next step of establishing the historical aspect of your psychological context.

Before elaborating, let me digress for one moment to remind you that the Beast is purely the voice of substance addiction. It is the voice of physical craving and is not connected with your past. Therefore, the Beast will not concern us here.

So put aside your Beast data, observe your Spoiled Child and/or your Insecure Child for a while, and review your journal carefully. Then look at specific examples and ask the question: "Where in my past did I actually behave (think, talk, react, etc.) like this?" Next find out with whom specifically in your life you were most likely to act this way. It is very helpful to know, for example, if it was only with your mother or your father that certain behavior took place.

By isolating the particular relationship(s) where you became spoiled or insecure, you can begin to assess what you were afraid of (e.g., abandonment, loss of love, abuse) or angry with (e.g., neglect, abuse, rejection). Remember, it was only as you grew older that these insecure or spoiled behaviors got relegated to the shadows of your mind.

The reason these spoiled or insecure tendencies usually become our secondary personalities is because adults generally view such behaviors as glaringly inappropriate and childish. We try hard to escape detection and humiliation by keeping our Child tendencies as private as possible. Every once in a while, if you are observant, you will catch a glimpse of someone's Child.

I recently saw a husband and wife at a shopping mall. It was obvious that the husband had become fatigued and cranky. Thinking no one was in earshot, he turned to his wife and whined, "My feet hurt. I don't want to shop anymore. It's not fair! You'd better leave now, or I'm really going to get [expletive deleted]!" Except for such times when one's guard is down, the Child is usually well-camouflaged from public view.

2. If withdrawal from your habit is chaotic, you will probably want to begin your psychological autobiography after the first wave of withdrawal has passed. If you are not dealing with a substance addiction, you may want to begin your psychological autobiography now. It can be part of your journal.

3. Using the same procedure you learned in Chapter 4, begin your autobiography by allowing yourself to free associate through your life. Start with your earliest memory, and let yourself eventually wind up in the present. Try not to anticipate or structure this task. Just begin and see what happens. The only structural suggestions I would make are that you use your conclusions (see Step 1 above) on where in the past and with whom such Childish tendencies flourished as focal points around which your associations can cluster. Also be sure to include your emotional reactions to the significant people and events of your past.

If, for example, you recall a time when your parents were fighting, try to recall and describe what you were feeling: *I was scared . . . really scared and angry. I was especially angry with my father. His voice was so loud! It made me feel so vulnerable. . . .*

Your thoughts may bounce from toddler to teen without rhyme or reason. Totally ignore the chronology of these events. Your only concern is with the emotional connections. These connections typically transcend time. You may, for example, have felt an intense fear the day you let go of your mother's hand and marched off to kindergarten, a pain that was re-experienced a few years later when you left for summer camp. Perhaps the same pain gripped you twenty years later on your honeymoon and now seems to be a component of why you use your habit to try to escape.

4. Once you have your document in hand — be it one page or one hundred pages — begin to digest it. Mull it over a while and let it affect you. You will never be able to do this at one sitting. Reread it often, allowing your reflections to roam freely. Each time you read, the threads that connect your past with your present will become more and more evident.

I remember the first time I looked through a telescope at the great Orion Nebula tucked into the sword of the constellation Orion the Hunter. At first glance all I saw was a disappointing smudge floating among the stars. My reaction was, "That's it?" Now, after many times at the eyepiece, the nebula has taken on wispy, ghostlike tendrils of glowing irridescent light with a sprinkling of faint stars backlighting the whole apparition — quite a heavenly masterpiece.

What happens is that the brain begins to accumulate perceptions — some obvious, some subliminal — and then adds these perceptions up, over time, to form an aggregate impression not apparent to the first-time observer. With your journal and your autobiography, the same thing happens. Over time you will notice things that you could not perceive initially. Be patient, be persistent, but most of all do not give up if nothing materializes after a few attempts. Allow your impressions to build up over time.

5 Although the psychological autobiography is a tool of follow-through, used mainly in your postcessation experiences, it is important to realize that it is a cumulative process of building impressions and insights. The earlier in your program you begin to write out and digest this material, the better. If you find yourself writing on and on, you can limit your autobiography by focusing only on where in the past and with whom you associate the voices of your Insecure Child and your Spoiled Child (see Step 1 above).

6 Jung felt that the only valid interpretation of a patient's dream was the one that seemed to click for the patient. The same will be true with your historical speculations. When something falls into place, you will experience the click of things coming together. You will come to glimpse many things, not all visible at first. Just keep turning things over and over again until something clicks for you.

One final word about perspective. Sometimes when the underlying history has involved severe abuse or psychological woundedness, counseling or some form of therapy can prove to be invaluable in gaining personal perspective. Group therapy is particularly powerful in dealing with addictive problems. There is nothing like hearing the stories of others who have gone through similar difficulties and suffered similar addictions to help us appreciate the human dimension to our problems. This dimension is particularly useful when the Insecure Child begins to become life's victim and cry, "Why me?"

There are many groups available, such as Alcoholics Anonymous, Narcotics Anonymous, Gamblers Anonymous, Overeaters Anonymous, Adult Children of Alcoholics, Al-Anon, and so on. Many community mental health centers offer programs or groups dealing with specific difficulties. Your state psychological association can provide further information on programs available in your area.

The psychological context is something that evolves and grows from your efforts to understand your entire experience, both conscious and unconscious. It is basically a process of putting your struggle into perspective. As you heal your habit, you will also begin a process of healing the woundedness that prompted you to adopt an addiction in the beginning.

About the Author

Dr. Joseph J. Luciani is a clinical psychologist in general private practice since 1977 in northern New Jersey. He has a Ph.D. in clinical psychology from the California School of Professional Psychology. A family man with two young children, he is an avid runner and an amateur astronomer.

LuraMedia Publications

Marjory Zoet Bankson, BRAIDED STREAMS: Esther and a Woman's Way of Growing (ISBN 0-931055-05-09)

SEASONS OF FRIENDSHIP: Naomi and Ruth as a Pattern (ISBN 0-931055-41-5)

Carolyn Stahl Bohler, PRAYER ON WINGS: A Search for Authentic Prayer (ISBN 0-931055-72-5)

Alla Renée Bozarth, WOMANPRIEST: A Personal Odyssey (ISBN 0-931055-51-2)

Judy Dahl, RIVER OF PROMISE: Two Women's Story of Love and Adoption (ISBN 0-931055-64-4)

Judith Duerk, CIRCLE OF STONES: Woman's Journey to Herself (ISBN 0-931055-66-0)

Lura Jane Geiger and Patricia Backman, BRAIDED STREAMS: Leader's Guide (ISBN 0-931055-09-1)

Lura Jane Geiger and Susan Tobias, SEASONS OF FRIENDSHIP: Leader's Guide (ISBN 0-931055-74-1)

Lura Jane Geiger, Sandy Landstedt, Mary Geckeler and Peggie Oury, ASTONISH ME, YAHWEH!: A Bible Workbook-Journal (ISBN 0-931055-01-6)

Kenneth L. Gibble, THE GROACHER FILE: A Satirical Exposé of Detours to Faith (ISBN 0-931055-55-5)

Ronna Fay Jevne, Ph.D. and Alexander Levitan, M.D., NO TIME FOR NONSENSE: Self-Help for the Seriously and Chronically Ill (ISBN 0-931055-63-6)

Ted Loder, EAVESDROPPING ON THE ECHOES: Voices from the Old Testament (ISBN 0-931055-42-3 HB; ISBN 0-931055-58-X PB)

GUERRILLAS OF GRACE: Prayers for the Battle (ISBN 0-931055-04-0)

NO ONE BUT US: Personal Reflections on Public Sanctuary (ISBN 0-931055-08-3)

TRACKS IN THE STRAW: Tales Spun from the Manger (ISBN 0-931055-06-7)

Joseph J. Luciani, Ph.D., HEALING YOUR HABITS: Introducing Directed Imagination, a Successful Technique for Overcoming Addictive Problems (ISBN 0-931055-71-7)

Jacqueline McMakin with Sonya Dyer, WORKING FROM THE HEART: For Those Who Hunger for Meaning and Satisfaction in Their Work (ISBN 0-931055-65-2)

Richard C. Meyer, ONE ANOTHERING: Biblical Building Blocks for a Healthy Group (0-931055-73-3)

Elizabeth O'Connor, SEARCH FOR SILENCE, Revised Edition (ISBN 0-931055-07-5)

Donna Schaper, A BOOK OF COMMON POWER: Narratives Against the Current (ISBN 0-931055-67-9)

SUPERWOMAN TURNS 40: The Story of One Woman's Intentions to Grow Up (ISBN 0-931055-57-1)

Renita Weems, JUST A SISTER AWAY: A Womanist Vision of Women's Relationships in the Bible (ISBN 0-931055-52-0)

LuraMedia is a company that searches for ways to encourage personal growth, shares the excitement of creative integrity, and believes in the power of faith to change lives.

7060 Miramar Rd., Suite 104
San Diego, California 92121